True Sea Stories

First published in 2005 by Usborne Publishing Ltd,
Usborne House, 83-85 Saffron Hill, London
EC1N 8RT, England.
www.usborne.com

A catalogue record for this title is available from
the British Library

UK ISBN 07460 58144

First published in America 2005
American ISBN 07945 07336

Printed in Great Britain

Designed by Brian Voakes
Illustrated by John Woodcock
Edited by Jane Chisholm
Cover design by Neil Francis
Cover photography © Joel W. Rogers/CORBIS
and Steve Wilkings/CORBIS
Series designer: Mary Cartwright

True Sea Stories

Henry Brook

Contents

Race the Savage Seas

The ocean-going yacht, *Suhaili*

Robin Knox-Johnston was all alone in the middle of the Atlantic Ocean when he noticed his boat was leaking. The lowest spaces in the craft, the bilges, were already ankle-deep and the water was still rising. His sturdy yacht, *Suhaili*, was built of the toughest Indian teak planks. But, if the bolts that clamped them together were coming apart, she could disintegrate at any second. The 27-year-old merchant seaman didn't panic or waste any time thinking of the dangers he faced. He was in a race around the world, and he'd come to terms with the possibility that it might cost him his life. Knox-Johnston concentrated on solving the problem.

He dropped sail to bring the boat to a halt, undressed and slipped into the sea. Diving underwater, he saw two gaping slits between the planks in the hull. They opened and closed like the gills of a great fish, as *Suhaili* rolled on the waves.

Back on deck, he took stock of the situation. The bolts were holding, but two of the planks had shifted out of position. To make them watertight he needed to fill the slits with shredded rope and cover them in tar – a process known as caulking. Sailors use a dry-dock for this kind of work, but Knox-Johnston didn't have that luxury. So instead, he took a handful of cotton and a screwdriver, swam down to the leak and spent thirty fruitless minutes trying to ram the fabric home. But it floated out every time the slits opened.

Undaunted, he sewed the cotton onto a strip of stiff canvas, then pushed a line of nails through the material. For two hours he toiled underwater, holding the canvas in place and driving the nails into the planks. It was exhausting, but it worked: the cotton held fast. Still, the job wasn't finished. Once *Suhaili* picked up speed, the canvas might be torn away by the force of rushing water. Knox-Johnston decided to protect his repair by covering it with a copper patch.

As he got ready to go in again, he saw a flicker at the corner of his eye and he hesitated. It was lucky he did. Scanning the water, he spotted a shark circling the boat. It was still there ten minutes later. Most people would have given in to despair at this point, but Knox-Johnston calmly went down to the cabin to fetch his gun. He threw some tissue paper onto the water to lure the shark to the surface. When it took the bait, he shot it in the head, then waited to see if the corpse would attract more predators. Satisfied that he was alone again, he dropped over the side and went back to work.

It was just another routine day at sea for Knox-Johnston, defending his lead in one of the world's greatest sailing races - the *Golden Globe*.

The idea for this particular race had come a year earlier. On May 28, 1967, Francis Chichester had completed his solo circumnavigation of the globe in *Gipsy Moth IV*, stopping only once to make repairs and take on supplies. His achievement had started a buzz in the world's sailing community. In every dockside yachting club, people were asking the same question: "Could anyone sail around the world alone, without stopping at all?"

It would take an exceptional sportsman to surpass the 65-year-old Chichester. He was a British national hero, with all the pluck and daring that are so admired by his countrymen. Nine years earlier, suffering with lung cancer, doctors had given him only six months to live. But Chichester defied them and sailed across the Atlantic, "to complete my cure," as he put it. Hungry for more ocean adventures, he voyaged around the world by way of the three capes: the Cape of Good Hope at the tip of South Africa, Cape Leeuwin on the west coast of Australia, and Cape Horn at the foot of South America. Because of strong winds and the curvature of the Earth, this is the quickest way for a yacht to circle the world - but it's also the riskiest. The route carried *Gipsy Moth IV* deep into the Southern Ocean, the deserted swathe of blue that runs around the lower southern hemisphere. Even the indomitable Chichester described this region as nightmarish. Storms could rage for weeks. Waves grew into walls of freezing water, rising up to a hundred feet high. Rounding Cape Horn was one of the most terrifying tasks; this jutting hook of land is pounded by huge seas and gale-force winds. It is a watery graveyard for sailors, strewn with wrecks and dreaded by the toughest navigators.

Chichester's cool-headed disregard for danger had kept him in the newspaper headlines. Of course, it might have helped that his yacht's sponsor was *The Sunday Times*. Eager to have another sailing adventure to report on, the newspaper came up with the idea of financing a race. During his voyage, Chichester had stopped in Sydney, Australia. Could any solo-sailor make the same, daring circumnavigation, but this time, non-stop and without assistance?

There were good reasons to think it was impossible. Most boats needed repairs after only a month or two at sea, and this voyage might take as long as a year. Would such prolonged loneliness drive a sailor mad? Communications were primitive compared to today. There was no internet, no GPS (Global Positioning System) or satellite navigation, not even an efficient telephone network. Apart from unreliable two-way radio sets, 1960s yachting technology had more in common with the days of

Captain Cook than with our own times. Knox-Johnston took an old-fashioned barometer to warn him of approaching storms; he'd borrowed it from a public bar.

But the non-stop title was a "holy grail" for sailors. Several yachtsmen were already making plans for the attempt when *The Sunday Times* announced details of their race. Sir Francis Chichester, recently knighted

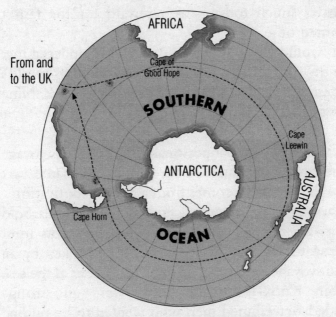

Map showing the route of the Golden Globe race

at Greenwich, was appointed race chairman.

The organizers knew it would be impossible for entrants to start at the same time and in the same location. There were simply too many people involved, all with different timetables. So they came up with a simple set of rules that would still create sporting tension. Anyone could take part – but on the condition that they left from a port on the British coast between June 1 and October 31 1968, accepted no help of any kind, and returned to the same port to finish. The first sailor home would win a statue of the globe and a place in history. To give the entrants an incentive to push themselves even harder, the newspaper offered a prize of £5000 – worth ten times as much today – as a reward for the fastest recorded time.

It would be a brutal and perilous undertaking: months of solitary confinement on the world's wildest seas, and constant, backbreaking work. Nine men set sail. Only one would make it home.

It takes an unusual personality to endure a voyage alone on the ocean. Lust for money and fame isn't enough. The drive comes from a deeper motivation – a yearning to pit oneself against incredible odds. Solo sailors are people who need to feel life at its most intense, to discover whether they'll be broken by an ocean voyage, or emerge from it as resilient as the sea. Robin Knox-Johnston's rivals were all strong-minded, determined men who wanted to be pushed to their limits. In this, at least, the Golden Globe would not disappoint them.

Chay Blyth and John Ridgway were ultra-fit SAS servicemen, who'd already proved their mettle by rowing across the Atlantic in an open boat. They were still in their twenties and, as part of their army training, had mastered survival techniques in jungles, deserts and arctic snowfields. Viewing the race as a simple test of stamina, they were undaunted by the enormity of what they were attempting. Both men had chosen small boats more suitable for gentle river cruising than a voyage around the world. They had limited yachting experience. Captain Ridgway had sailed a few hundred miles in practice runs around the UK. Sergeant Blyth, a cheery but resolute man, had only managed about six miles of solo sailing by the time he joined the race.

Bernard Moitessier was an enigmatic, middle-aged yachtsman who loved the sea with a passion. He was already a "Cape Horner" – having sailed his steel-plated craft, *Joshua*, around the Cape in 1965. Moitessier had written two bestsellers about his voyages, and the success of these books in his native France had given him a taste of money and fame. But the easy living and celebrity carnival depressed him. He was longing to get out on the water again.

Bill King was 57, a farmer and retired submarine captain who mortgaged his farm to pay for his boat, *Galway Blazer II*. He was no stranger to risk: King had been a test pilot for the first catapult system that launched aircraft from moving ships. Another navy man, Commander Nigel Tetley, was having breakfast in bed on *Victress*, the catamaran he called home, when he saw the advertisement for the race. He turned to his wife and asked if she'd mind him sailing around the world. Despite worries for his safety alone on the seas, she pledged her support. The other entrants were Loick Fougeron, a friend of Moitessier's who lived in Casablanca, an Italian named Alex Carozzo and an electronics engineer from Somerset, Donald Crowhurst.

Of all the yachts, Moitessier's and King's were considered the fastest. The underdog for the race was a scruffy yacht that had been bolted together by Indian carpenters. It was captained by a square-jawed British merchant navy officer... named Robert Knox-Johnston.

Knox-Johnston left Falmouth on June 14, a week after Blyth and two weeks after Ridgway. He knew *Suhaili* was the slowest boat in the competition, but he was hoping that speed wouldn't be the only factor in winning. *Suhaili* might only cruise at walking pace, but on previous voyages she had proved to be as strong as a tank, and Knox-Johnston trusted her seaworthiness. If he was lucky, her plodding - but consistent - performance could be an advantage over the faster but flimsier boats.

In keeping with his simple approach to race tactics, Knox-Johnston's dietary requirements were extremely straightforward. He stashed over a thousand cans of ready-cooked food in *Suhaili*'s hold, including 144 cans of baked beans and 216 of corned beef. The prospect of eating the same meal for ten months didn't seem to bother him. Leaving Falmouth, *Suhaili* wallowed in the water under the weight of her cargo. In the first week, she was only making about 130km (80 miles) a day - compared with the 240km (150 miles) that Bill King was confident of sailing. But Knox-Johnston's hopes for *Suhaili* were well-founded. While he pressed southwards, the ocean began to take her toll on the other boats, and their captains.

John Ridgway had confronted all manner of terrors in his military career. He had been an officer in an elite parachute regiment and was strong in mind and body. But the sea exposes any hidden human weakness. This was Ridgway's first solo voyage and he hated being alone. After six weeks with only the waves for company, he was overwhelmed by a crushing sense of isolation. Instead of enjoying the solitude, the sense of union between boat and sea, he saw his situation as a self-made hell. To add to his worries, his fair-weather yacht was cracking up around him. Nobody had dared tell the forthright Ridgway that taking a family cruiser around the three Capes would be suicidal. After all, this was a man who'd rowed across the Atlantic. But Ridgway knew he was in trouble when he saw the deck bulging around the plates that held his boat's mast in position. He realized that if he hit a storm, the deck could split open with fatal results. So he headed off to Brazil, the first man to leave the race.

His sergeant, Blyth, pressed on as far as South Africa. But after sailing 14,000 km (9,000 miles), he too accepted that his boat was no match for the savagery of the Southern Ocean. He retired from the race, though his voyage was a remarkable achievement for a novice yachtsman.

Bill King was knocked down - rolled over - by a colossal wave that tore off his masts. Shocked by the might of the sea, he crept into Cape Town in his broken boat.

Fougeron, having weathered his first hurricane south of the equator, was knocked down too and decided once was enough. He docked at St. Helena. Carozzo was a victim of stress: he suffered a bleeding stomach ulcer and was rescued in the Atlantic by the Portuguese navy.

This left Moitessier, Tetley and Crowhurst. They all sailed late, and began chasing after *Suhaili* in their faster craft.

Sailing out of the Atlantic around the Cape of Good Hope and deep into the Southern Ocean, Knox-Johnston battled against storms and injury to protect his lead. Aside from the problems with the leak, he had discovered his water tanks were contaminated with brine. He was wondering if he had enough cans of fruit juice on board to keep him alive. His hands were chapped and bloody from hard work and he had burned his left eye with battery acid when a freak wave unfooted him. The pain was so sharp he couldn't sleep and he thought he might lose his sight in that eye. Durban and medical attention were nearby. But that would disqualify him. He decided the sight of one eye was a price worth paying to win the race.

There are more sinister difficulties for the solo

navigator than physical pain, as Ridgway had discovered. Knox-Johnston's radio was so weak it was useless for much of his voyage – the pub barometer was more reliable. For a period of five months, he was out of sight of land and had no contact with another human being. Hunched over in his tiny cabin – walled with sodden clothes, torn maps and creaking boards – there was time to daydream. Knox-Johnston began visualizing his own drowning. *Suhaili* had been knocked down once before, so he knew what it was like to feel his world corkscrew and explode under a wave. He imagined the black water gushing in and the icy sting of it on his skin, the roaring in his ears and the screams... his own screams.

But that mysterious quality that makes a solo sailor ran deep in Knox-Johnston. He scolded himself for his gloomy thoughts and went back to work. There was a race to be won. At New Zealand he anchored in a deserted bay. His newspaper sponsor had a journalist waiting on the islands and Knox-Johnston sent him a message via some fishermen he'd hailed. Although the journalist wasn't allowed to hand over any supplies, he told Knox-Johnston the latest race news. The pack was closing fast: Tetley and Crowhurst were still in the game and Moitessier was only weeks behind. Knowing that he had to protect every hour of his lead, Knox-Johnston set sail the next morning.

By now, he had been at sea for over 160 days, weathered hurricane-force storms and extreme fatigue and still come out fighting. Tackling fierce waves all the way across to South America, Knox-Johnston rounded Cape Horn on January 17, 1969. His hands were blistered and torn and his boat scruffier than ever, but he was smiling. The merchant navy sailor had come further than any other non-stop navigator; he downed a whiskey to celebrate.

Entering the Atlantic once more, *Suhaili* headed north, making for home. Whatever happened, Knox-Johnston was sure he would finish the circumnavigation. The only nagging doubt in his mind was his position in the race. Could the Frenchman – as he called Moitessier – snatch the lead from him? Knox-Johnston was so desperate to win, he pushed *Suhaili* as hard as he dared, never relaxing for a moment. As before, gruelling work was the best distraction from his worries.

The Frenchman had worries too, but they were quite different from his opponent's. On March 18, Moitessier sailed into Cape Town and announced his decision to quit the race. He had rounded Cape Horn just behind *Suhaili*, and would have overtaken her easily, barring any accident. But the months alone on the ocean had made Moitessier question his priorities. He was more at home on the sea than on dry land. It was the sailing that was important to him, not winning a race. If he returned home he would be treated like a hero. Out on the waves, Moitessier realized that this was the last thing he wanted. So he rejected certain glory and set sail for Tahiti, to "save his soul" – as he put it, in a closing letter to *The*

Sunday Times.

So, the ocean claimed another contestant, in a style nobody could have predicted. But there was even stranger news to come.

From his sporadic radio reports, the British newspapers estimated Donald Crowhurst to be somewhere in the South Atlantic, poised to pass Tetley and even to catch up with Knox-Johnston. It was true he was in the Atlantic Ocean. In fact, he'd never left it.

Crowhurst had been sailing around in circles for months, making false position reports and waiting for the other contestants to arrive for the home straight. He planned to slip back into the race, tricking everyone into believing he'd sailed around the world. At first, this devious scheme was at least rational – Crowhurst was clever enough to make his faked navigational log look convincing. But it soon veered into outright lunacy, as the electrical wizard lost control of his mind.

He had staked everything on winning the Golden Globe: his house was mortgaged and his company and all his assets were on the line. Worse than this, he had gambled his reputation as an inventor and designer on the race outcome. Crowhurst was 36, had a brilliant mind and liked to let people know it. He had designed his own boat, *Teignmouth Electron*, and equipped it with groundbreaking new safety and navigational devices. There was even a rudimentary computer set up in the cabin, to coordinate his electrical innovations. Before

Crowhurst sailed, the newspapers described the ex-RAF charmer as a "dark horse" who might smash the records with his super-boat.

But the reality was quite different. *Teignmouth Electron* had been poorly designed and shoddily built. Nothing was ready on time and the boat should never have left port. True enough, there was an impressive tangle of cables snaking across the floor of the cabin, connecting all corners of the craft with the computer. But the wires disappeared under a cushion, ending in a tangled heap. They hadn't been connected to the computer because it didn't exist. It was still only at the design stage, another scheme in Crowhurst's mind.

After two weeks at sea he knew his boat wouldn't survive the Southern Ocean. Too ashamed to go home, he drifted off the coast of Brazil for months, making his false reports. By the time Knox-Johnston and Tetley were fighting their way up from Cape Horn, Crowhurst was so wracked with guilt and self-disgust his mind snapped. One night he climbed up on deck, took a last look at the pitiless ocean and stepped over the side. His boat was recovered a few weeks later. The logbook told the whole story: Crowhurst's confession recorded in a feverish scrawl.

Commander Tetley had heard the reports of Crowhurst's amazing progress on his radio, and was rigging *Victress* under full sail. If only he had known he was racing against a stationary madman, he might have nursed his boat instead. *Victress* was already damaged – her port hull was cracked and taking water – but the brave navy man drove her on. While he was dozing in the cabin one night, he heard a terrible crunch. The port bow had snapped off and holed the main hull as it went. *Victress* was sinking. Tetley struggled into a raft and was picked up the next day by an Italian tanker, after eight months of hard racing. His crash site was only two weeks' sail from home.

On April 22, 1969, a tubby, dirty yacht lumbered into Falmouth docks. Officers from the Customs Authorities moored alongside and greeted the solitary, bearded sailor with the regulation question: "Where from?"

"Falmouth," answered Knox-Johnston, smiling with delight. He had already been tipped off by friends in a waiting motor launch that the race was his. After 312 days at sea, and 48,000km (30,000 miles), the *Suhaili* tortoise had won the Golden Globe and – even more remarkable – was the only boat to finish the course.

The *Birkenhead* Heroes

The paddle steamer
HMS Birkenhead

Those who survived that night would never forget the sound of the horses, screaming as they were herded over the side. Major Seton had ordered his officers to drive their animals into the sea, in the hope some might swim to shore. But the sharks were waiting. Only five out of eighteen horses made it to safety, to the sandy beaches along Danger Point just two miles distant.

The cry of the horses was just one of the dreadful sounds coming from the wreck. Men were screaming too, as they died, drowning in the flooded forward sections of the huge, stricken ship, crushed by falling debris and trapped behind bolted hatches. The majority of the soldiers had been asleep when the hull tore open, and those who staggered to the main deck were half-dressed and startled. They were amazed by what they saw. *HMS Birkenhead* was breaking apart. Although it was a clear, fair night, her iron keel buckled and bulged under the black waves. She was caught on an uncharted reef. If the ship couldn't float free, the ocean swell would soon grind her to pieces against the rocks.

Down below, the stokers in the engine room watched as the metal plates of the hull crumpled and folded before them. A second later the iron wall ripped open and the sea rushed in through a new gash in the ship's side. Most of the men died instantly, but a few managed to scramble up escape ladders and find their captain. He took the news bravely, but understood the significance of their reports. With her boilers flooded, his ship couldn't steer. They were trapped on the reef. Already, the deck planks groaned and splintered as the prow dropped away under the weight of flooded compartments. The proud funnel, once a symbol of the *Birkenhead*'s unvanquishable power on the waves, swayed and fell, killing dozens of soldiers as it smashed into the deck.

With a shudder, the stern lifted fifty feet into the air. Hundreds of men had gathered there with their commander, Major Seton, and his officers, assembling on the poop deck in regimental formation and waiting for orders. Most of them were raw recruits, still in their teens. They'd never experienced the shock and horror of combat; the hard truth was that some of them were about to die. Dozens were already injured and had to be supported by their friends. They were barefoot and their uniforms looked ragged and incomplete. In the mad rush to the main deck, there had only been time to snatch a tunic or a nightshirt from their hammocks. But still the soldiers held their ranks, almost as perfectly as they had on the parade ground a few weeks earlier.

There was a sudden cry from the rigging above them: "She's about to go under, boys. Swim to the boats and save yourselves." It was the ship's captain, calling out a warning as he prepared to dive. A murmur ran through the throng of men. In the minutes after the collision, Major Seton, had ordered all the women and children into the lifeboats. The ship's crew could only lower three boats – the other five on board had been damaged by the crash or their release mechanisms were faulty. But all the passengers had escaped safely. The three boats were circling a few hundred yards from the wreck, waiting to see if the *Birkenhead* would stay afloat.

Every man on the poop deck must have had the same thought: if he could only get into a boat he had a chance to live. When the stern crashed into the sea they would be sucked under and drowned – or meet a worse end if the sharks got them – but if they could reach the boats...

"Listen to me, men," Major Seton called above the terrible noise of the wreck. "I want you to maintain your positions. There's no room for us in the boats and the women and children will be endangered if we try to join them. I want every last one of you to hold fast."

The major was ordering them to make the greatest sacrifice, to lay down their lives so that others might survive. He was asking them to die bravely, standing in their lines. Poised above the sea on the tilting, creaking deck, the men on the *Birkenhead* had only seconds to make their decision.

Since the day of her launch, in December 1845, the paddle-steamer *HMS Birkenhead* had been an impressive ship. Her designer, John Laird, was convinced that the new "irons" were the way of the future and he wanted his creation to stand as an example to the diehards who insisted ships should be constructed of wood.

"My ship won't rot," he told his critics, "she won't warp, swell or shrink, won't be chewed up by beetles or worms and she won't burn."

"Yes, but will she float?" they replied in scorn.

In fact, the iron ships had an advantage over their wooden rivals when it came to maintaining buoyancy: watertight compartments. Designers positioned the welded bulkheads running between decks into iron cells. This was to prevent sea water from flooding the whole ship if one part of the hull was holed. Iron bulkheads couldn't guarantee a ship's survival – the *Titanic*, built in 1911, had sixteen watertight cells and she still went down – but they were an undoubted safety improvement.

Iron had another advantage over wood: it was easily available. Britain's forests were seriously depleted. Anyone who visits the wide open plains of the New Forest today might wonder what happened to all the trees: the answer is they were cut down for Henry VIII's naval carpenters. As a result, shipbuilders were forced to import wood from Europe and it was often of poor quality.

Laird rightly predicted the inevitable switch from wood to metal ships. But, like many people with fresh ideas, he had to wait a long time before his views were accepted. He wanted the *Birkenhead* to be a warship, heavily armed and lightly manned. At first, the British admirals were enthusiastic about his plan. But when they were mocked in the press for commissioning an untested iron battleship they got cold feet. After keeping the *Birkenhead* in dock for a year and a half they decided to use their new purchase as a troop transporter instead. To give her 500 or more passengers quicker access around the lower decks, navy engineers cut doors into the bulkheads. This clumsy modification of Laird's plans would cost dearly in human lives.

For almost two years the *Birkenhead* served as a fast and comfortable troopship. Then, on January 7, 1852, she sailed from Cork, Ireland, bound for Port Elizabeth on the southern coast of Africa. She was carrying around 690 passengers and crew, 500 of them army reinforcements for the British colonial war against the Xhosa people. But the soldiers' courage would be tested long before they reached any battlefield.

The passengers' first ordeal was a winter storm that pounded the iron ship for ten days and nights. It was so violent the men below decks were convinced they would drown. They groaned in their hammocks, trying to ignore the sickening lurch of the ship on every wave. Up on the main deck, sailors at the stern could see the huge rudder lift clear out of the water each time the *Birkenhead* pitched forward. Even lifelong mariners were seasick and the jarring movements brought on contractions for the six pregnant women on board. Three babies were born during that storm, and three women died of internal bleeding before giving birth.

At last the *Birkenhead* steamed clear of the bad weather and anchored off the island of Madeira to take on supplies. The ship was bathed in sunshine and soldiers who had never left their homeland had their first look at the balmy tropics. Cruising down the west coast of Africa, the ship made up some of the time lost to the storm, calling at Sierra Leone and St. Helena before docking in Simon's Bay, close to Cape Town on February 23. All that remained of her voyage was the two-day passage to Port Elizabeth, further up the coast. Before leaving Simon's Bay she took on horses for the officers, more coal and seven new passengers, while some of the men who had never recovered from the rough weather were carried to a hospital on shore.

In the early evening of February 25, *HMS Birkenhead* got up steam and set out to sea again. Because fresh troops were needed urgently, the master, Captain Robert Salmond, had orders to reach his destination as fast as possible. He plotted a direct course that hugged the rocky coastline rather than steering for deeper water. But this was not a reckless decision, despite the heightened risks of reefs and tides. Salmond was an experienced and cautious mariner, who came from a family that had dedicated themselves to life at sea. His father, four brothers, and even one of his own sons, had died while on naval duty, and the safety of his ship was his chief priority. Salmond's navigator had studied detailed maps of the hidden reefs and rocks in the area and approved the route. For added security, the captain stationed two of his crew at the prow to act as lookouts, and had a third man taking constant soundings of the sea's depth with a lead weight and line.

Chugging along at cruising speed, the *Birkenhead* was so close to land the men standing on her decks could see signal fires flickering in the hills as night fell. Satisfied that his ship was in no danger, Salmond passed command to one of his officers and retired to his cabin. By midnight, most of the passengers and crew had followed his example and were fast asleep. The only noise was the rhythmic churning of the paddle wheels in the surf and the soft voices of a few officers and men who had stayed up to take the air and chat.

Just before two o'clock in the morning, the *Birkenhead* was slicing through the waters around Danger Point, about 110 km (70 miles) from Simon's Bay. She was two miles off the shore, in water about eighty feet deep. According to the charts, the channel ahead of her was free of obstacles – but the charts lied. Rising up from the seabed, a great crag of rock blocked her path, its sharp peak hidden just inches below the waves. If the ship had been only a few feet to the north or south of this rock, she would have surged past in ignorance of the danger. But the *Birkenhead* ran straight onto the crag, ripping a great hole in her hull and slamming to a sudden halt.

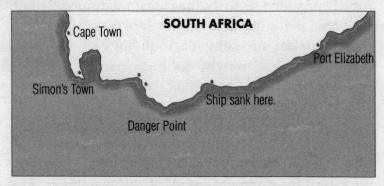

Map showing the crash site of the *Birkenhead*

Sergeant John Drake was one of the soldiers chatting on the main deck. The first thing he knew of the collision was when he was thrown suddenly off his feet. Every board and rivet in the ship sounded as if it was exploding. Through the thick, oak planks of the deck, Drake could hear screams from the forward compartment of the troop deck: the bow was flooding and soldiers drowned where they lay in their hammocks. Drake picked himself up and sprinted to the poop deck, where the officers could

30

be found. He was a career soldier, a tough and resourceful man who had earned promotion from the ranks by defending a captured ship against her mutinous crew. While Drake had been sleeping, six Spanish sailors had attacked him with a knife and club. Bleeding and stunned, Drake had fought back, killing two of his assailants and beating the others unconscious. Drake was a survivor and he was determined to help save the *Birkenhead*.

Captain Salmond was on deck minutes after the collision. He collected his officers as they emerged from below and coolly instructed them to report on the damage and to send word to stop the engines. He had every confidence that the *Birkenhead* was intact and seaworthy: if the flooding could be confined to the first watertight section of the ship, she would not sink. But despite this he ordered Drake to escort the women and children to the boats. After all, there was no reason not to take every available precaution.

When Major Seton reached the main deck he gave a general order for all troops to assemble there and spoke calmly with his officers. Seton was a striking figure amid the chaos of the struggling ship. Dressed in full uniform, complete with regimental sword, he impressed everyone with his self-confidence and control. From a family of Scottish Highlanders, the 38-year-old major was much loved both by the officers and men. He was a great scholar and spoke a dozen languages fluently. But above all he was an army man. He studied the crisis around him with a professional eye and acted quickly to restore order.

Seton dispatched a party of men to each boat station, then began organizing the shocked, bedraggled troops into their drill positions. The major wanted to reassure his soldiers, and believed the discipline of the parade ground was the best way to achieve it. He also had the sense to think of their possible rescue, and asked an officer to fire the ship's guns to alert people on the land to the ship's distress. The ammunition was sodden, but the officer managed to find some rockets and fired them into the night sky. They illuminated a shocking scene of disaster.

The men trying to free the lifeboats had discovered that their fixing pins and catches were either rusted or painted into place. They struggled desperately to launch the boats, but on the rocking decks it proved impossible. Only three craft made it into the water. Major Seton quickly supervised the embarkation of the terrified women and children.

As the boats touched the water, Captain Salmond gave an order that would have terrible consequences for his ship. With every swell of the waves, the *Birkenhead* grated and cracked on the rock. In an attempt to escape the reef's clasp he ordered the engines into reverse. But, as the mighty paddles slowly began to revolve, they dragged the ship over the crag, opening another tear in her iron hull. Instead of saving his ship, Salmond had destroyed her. The engine room – the largest compartment below decks – quickly flooded and the ship settled even deeper on the rock. With two compartments now open to the sea – and the others already weakened by the doors that had been cut into them – the *Birkenhead* was doomed.

Fifteen minutes after the collision, Major Seton and his troops watched in horror as the bow broke away and the funnel crashed into the deck. One moment their ship had been cruising across the ocean, seemingly invincible and only hours from port. Now she was a wreck, splintered, broken and sinking. The scene drove some of the men into panic, but Seton kept his composure. He ordered his soldiers to the poop deck, where they fell back into neat lines.

It was another five minutes before the final death throes of the *Birkenhead*. In that time, the soldiers waiting with Seton had to make their choice – to swim for the boats or go down with the ship. It was the ultimate test of their heroism.

The men made their decision, and held their ranks. As the stern plunged into the sea, they shook hands with one another and watched the waves sweeping over the deck. At least two hundred soldiers sank below the surface in drill position, rather than jeopardize the safety of the lifeboats.

John Drake was one of them. He felt the water close over his head and the suction of the sinking ship tugging at his feet. For more than a minute he was lost in the underwater shadows. But the *Birkenhead* was in shallow waters, and when the vortex subsided Drake found he could swim to the surface. He came up spluttering and coughing for air, straight into a scene of carnage. The waves were covered with bits of broken wood, dying men and the thrashing fins of rapacious sharks. Drake noticed a wide plank bobbing next to him and clambered aboard. He had pledged to stay clear of the lifeboats, but perhaps he could float to shore on this makeshift raft.

There was a whimper in the darkness next to him. Drake pulled an exhausted soldier out of the water and helped him to straddle the plank. The man barely had the strength to hold on, but Drake gripped his hand and told him they could paddle their way to land. Suddenly the plank smashed against a rock and snapped. Drake fought his way to the surface again, but the soldier he'd rescued had disappeared, perhaps taken by a shark. Refusing to give up hope, Drake swam across to where the ship's main mast was poking out of the waves, and pulled himself up into the rigging.

He was still there the next afternoon when the schooner *Lioness* came to his rescue.

Drake was one of the lucky ones: the wreck of the *Birkenhead* claimed around 445 lives; only 190 men survived. The soldiers who came up from the sinking poop deck stood little chance against the prowling sharks. A few managed to swim to shore or cling to anything that would float – pieces of the ship's decks, dining tables, even bales of hay that had been stowed below for the horses. Those who were strong enough to reach the coast faced another hazard before they could rest on dry land. Banks of thick seaweed blocked the beaches, and the tired men had to clamber across or swim around them to find the shore. They huddled on the sand, naked and freezing, waiting to be saved.

Aside from the sacrifice made by the troops on the poop deck, there were other tales of heroism that night. A young soldier, Ensign Russell, was part of the crew for one of the lifeboats. When he spotted a boy struggling in the water, he immediately jumped to his feet and offered to give up his seat. A sailor hauled the exhausted boy into the boat and Russell, true to his word, dived over the side. He was a strong swimmer and kept up with the rowers, but a few minutes after surrendering his place he was yanked below by a shark.

When word of the disaster reached Cape Town, the British authorities sent a steamer to scour the coast for survivors. They found around sixty men who had swum ashore; one of them had staggered onto a beach, to find his horse waiting there for him. Seton, Salmond and most of the other officers went down with the ship.

The loss of the *Birkenhead* represents perhaps the greatest example of bravery in the history of the British army. At least 200 men were willing to face death rather than endanger the lifeboats. In May 1852, a court martial in Portsmouth cleared the ship's officers of any blame for the accident and praised their conduct. The popular press was more effusive and expressed the mood of the nation when it described the *Birkenhead* troops as heroes. Their sacrifice was recognized worldwide.

There is a simple, stone memorial to the *Birkenhead* dead by the lighthouse on Danger Point. And, at low tide, the rock that sank her is still clearly visible above the waves.

The Queen's Dragon

Sir Francis Drake's coat-of-arms. The Latin motto reads:
Greatness from small beginnings.

The raiders had been hacking their way through thick jungle for days and they were exhausted. Their local guides were Cimarrons, escaped slaves, hardened to the breathless heat and humidity of the rainforest. They thought nothing of marching for hours in these conditions, without rest or water. In contrast, the force of 18 bedraggled English sailors looked almost dead on their feet. Months of skirmishing along the Caribbean coast had left them battle-weary and ragged. Some were sick and trembling with the yellow fever that had already killed so many of their crewmates. Their captain, Francis Drake, had lost his elder brother, Joseph, to the disease. Another brother, John, had been shot dead in a gunfight during an attack on a Spanish frigate. Drake reflected on how much he'd sacrificed, and how very little he'd gained, since arriving in the Spanish colonies of Central America.

But no hardship or family loss could sway the captain from his plans. Only a day's march away, a mule train loaded with gold and silver ingots was snaking its way towards the coast. Drake was determined to ambush and steal this bullion. Even though every single step was torture, he urged his men on.

Drake looked up and saw the leader of the Cimarrons beckoning. The man led him over a hill, to a clearing with a solitary tree at its heart. Taller than any ship's mast the captain had ever seen, the tree had a platform built around its top like a crow's nest. There were steps cut into the trunk and the Cimarron gestured to the captain to climb. When he reached the platform, Drake looked east to the bay where his ships were anchored. It was the gateway to the Atlantic and to his distant home. Then he turned and, for the first time in his life, Francis Drake glimpsed the Pacific. The high platform in the jungle offered views of two oceans, separated by the 40 mile strip of Panama. Despite all his recent sufferings, the sight of the world's largest body of water made Drake's heart race. Few Englishmen had ever seen this ocean and none had voyaged across it.

"I will sail that sea, one day," Drake promised himself. "For my monarch, for my glory... and for my purse."

The captain's tenacity and ambition paid off: he left Panama with enough booty to make him one of England's richest men. His wealth and daring earned him an invitation to Queen Elizabeth's court and the nickname *El Draque* – the Dragon – from the Spanish king. His reputation as a swashbuckler was spreading to every port in the known world, but his greatest adventure was still to come.

Drake's fame and achievements are all the more remarkable considering his origins. He was born in Devon in 1540, in a stone barn his family shared with farm animals. After a series of public brawls, Drake's father fled the county and the young Francis was packed off to live with his cousin, John Hawkins, in Plymouth. It was here that Drake discovered the sea, and a passion for it that would shape the rest of his life. The Hawkins family owned several merchant ships and Francis Drake sailed with them while still in his early teens. He was quick to learn the tricks of the trade – legal or otherwise.

In the Elizabethan age, one man's piracy was another man's patriotism. If the Hawkins' ships plundered a vessel from Spain – a country on the brink of war with England over religious differences – the authorities simply turned a blind eye. The Spanish ambassador in London complained to the Queen about English pirates. But, while she might nod her head in sympathy, if their actions didn't interfere with her own political interests she was reluctant to reprimand them. And, if they happened to donate half their plunder from their raids to her coffers, so much the better. Official indifference towards attacks on Spanish shipping and ports meant that pirates thrived.

The Hawkins family had other skills, more horrible than piracy. They were slavers, plying back and forth between the coasts of West Africa and the new colonies in the Caribbean. Drake joined these voyages, working his way up the order of command until he was made captain of a ship. During a series of attacks against the Spanish in Mexico, he developed the technique of striking hard and running to sea before troop reinforcements could arrive. He also mastered the fine art of saving his own skin, deserting John Hawkins in the thick of battle when it became clear his ship was overburdened. Hawkins had to abandon 100 men on the beach – to face a lifetime of slavery in the Peruvian silver mines – because of Drake's hasty exit. But the Dragon wasn't cowardly. Instead, he was a ruthless commander who put little value on the lives of others. While this characteristic was dangerous for his crews, it proved immensely lucrative for those who invested in his voyages. Although in polite company they dismissed him as a violent adventurer, the Queen and her counsellors always accepted his loot. When Drake came to them with an idea to plunder the rich towns along the west coast of the Americas, they listened carefully to his proposal.

The Queen's Dragon

In November, 1577, a fleet of five ships and 170 "men and boyes" left Plymouth under the joint command of Drake, his friend, Thomas Doughty, and another captain, John Wynter. The flagship, Drake's *Pelican*, had 18 guns and was the largest vessel. This ship later became more famous under a new name: the *Golden Hinde*. She was around 80 feet long and 20 feet wide; a small craft considering she was bound for the other side of the world.

Cruising into the English Channel, the crews believed they were bound for Alexandria, Egypt, where the ships were to pick up a cargo of currants. But this was a whisper that had been put about by Elizabeth's spies at court, to deliberately deceive the Spanish. Drake's true mission was to sail into the Pacific by way of the Strait of Magellan, and seek out trading possibilities along the coast of Chile and Peru. The English were jealous of Spain's dominance in South America: it was a continent rich in gold, silver, precious gems and exotic animal hides. If Drake could establish bases along the coast and win his country new land he would earn the Queen's blessing. National pride was also at stake: it was about time an Englishman conquered the Pacific. Court officials and dignitaries were encouraged to invest in the mission as a patriotic duty – with the financial sweetener of Drake's reputation as a pillager and pirate. The captain always came home with a ship full of swag to be split between himself and his backers. Elizabeth let her dragon off his leash, wondering what treasure he would bring back to her from the Spanish territories.

Drake sailed south, stopping for fresh water and firewood along the coast of Africa and at the Cape Verde Islands. He seized any ships he encountered, ransacking their stores and press-ganging their crews into his fleet. It didn't take long for his men to realize they weren't going to Egypt – and that their captain had other cargo in mind than currants. When a sailor questioned Doughty about their mission, he was told their welcome home would be all the warmer if they were weighed down with gold.

Leaving dry land behind them, the sailors gossiped about the terrors that lay ahead. Their first destination was the strait, a slim channel of powerful tides and needle-sharp rocks at the bottom of South America. In Drake's time, no European had sailed further south than this point – anything beyond it was blank space on the map. Many sailors still believed that ships simply fell off the edge of the world when they entered these waters – or were swallowed by sea monsters.

The crews had other reasons to be miserable. In the 16th century, a long voyage at sea usually resulted in the deaths of at least half the men. There were no hammocks in those days, so the sailors curled up to sleep on damp, filthy boards, leaving them vulnerable to colds and rheumatism. Their food was limited to rice, fish or a sort of dried bread, known as ship's biscuit, with the occasional luxury such as a turtle or sheep snatched from a foreign shore. The lack of vitamins in their diet – particularly vitamin C – led to outbreaks of a disease called scurvy, when whole crews could sicken and die in bone-cracking agony. Water was another problem. Elizabethan sailors rarely washed - they usually only had one set of clothes to last the whole voyage - and their idea of personal hygiene was relaxed, to put it mildly. Water stocks

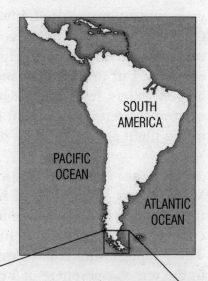

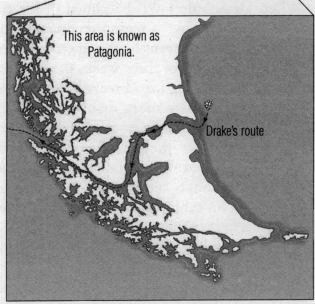

Map showing Drake's route through the Strait of Magellan, at the southern tip of South America

were easily contaminated. It was safer to drink beer –
the brewing process killed germs – and sailors were
often provided with up to eight pints of foaming ale
each day. But this couldn't protect them against the
biggest killers: fever and plague. In the tight, airless
spaces between decks, a man could pick up a cough
in the night and be dead by morning.

Ignorance was the source of other dangers.
Without any knowledge of meteorology, navigators
thought the winds propelling their ships were
controlled by vengeful gods or the spells of sorcerers.
These superstitions could have terrible consequences
in the tense atmosphere of a cramped ship.

When Drake's fleet was becalmed in the tropical
heat of the doldrums – a region renowned today for
its erratic wind patterns – the men wondered if
they'd been cursed. For three weeks the crews sizzled
on the planks, waiting for a breeze. A dead calm tests
the nerves of a sailor more than the perils of any
hurricane. In the grip of a storm, everyone is so busy
trying to stay alive they have no time to think.
Trapped on a sea as still as glass, even a patient man
can give in to doubts and begin to lose his mind.

Fuming in his cabin, Drake was sure he knew why
the fleet was becalmed. It was all the fault of his
fellow commander, Doughty. The man was surely a
necromancer – a magician in the black arts.

In the Elizabethan age these accusations were not
uncommon. Baffled by the natural world, men
believed witchcraft was the cause of every disaster or

accident. Whether or not Drake really believed Doughty was a witch, he certainly despised his former friend. From the beginning of the voyage he had resented Doughty's influence and the circle of noblemen who escorted him. Drake, born in a stone hut, was convinced these educated courtiers looked down on him. Perhaps they were even plotting to take control of his fleet.

After a trivial incident with one of the *Pelican*'s trumpeters – there was some horseplay and Doughty slapped the man as a joke – Drake decided to act. He removed the puzzled nobleman from his command and isolated him away from his supporters on the smallest ship in the fleet, the *Swan*. The enraged Doughty openly criticized Drake in front of the *Swan*'s crew, reminding them he was a commander of the same rank and could prove this by force if necessary. He would come to regret this outburst.

For four months the fleet followed the coast of Brazil southwards, landing occasionally to forage for wood and water. They were pounded by sudden storms – Doughty's sorcery, hissed Drake – and lost two men in confrontations with hostile local tribes. Poor Doughty was blamed for everything. Finally, perhaps wanting to reassert his power over his men in these fearful waters, Drake ordered a court martial. On June 30, 1578, the entire company assembled on the beach at Port San Julian, Argentina, and Drake charged Doughty with mutiny.

Drake immediately turned the trial into a test of his leadership. Ignoring Doughty's request to be judged in front of a proper court in England, Drake challenged the jury either to condemn the upstart courtier, or to abandon the voyage and return home in disgrace. This brought howls from the watching sailors. Drake had already promised every man more gold than he could carry once they entered the Pacific. When the jury heard the captain of the *Swan* describing Doughty's rebellious outburst, the case was lost. Doughty was found guilty and Drake immediately sentenced him to death.

The Dragon offered the condemned man a choice: the firing squad or the executioner. Doughty chose the latter. On July 2, Drake sat down for a meal with the man he had destroyed, said some prayers with him and watched as he laid his chin on the block. As Doughty's head rolled from his body, Drake snatched it up and held it aloft.

"This is the end of traitors," he roared, to cheers from the sailors. The Dragon had sacrificed the life of one of his fellow commanders to give his crews a sense of unity and purpose. But, as they walked away from the scene of the execution, some of them must have wondered if it would be their turn next.

Over the next month, Drake tried to restore the courage of his men and repaired the weathered ships. Only three were seaworthy: the *Marigold*, the *Elizabeth* and the *Pelican*. By mid-August they reached the opening of the dreaded strait. With their hearts in their mouths, the sailors entered the narrow channel of swirling tides and hidden rocks. For two weeks, they navigated between mountains, passing islands flocked with shrieking birds and weaving around jagged outcrops. At last, on September 6, they entered the Pacific. Their trial in the Strait was over.

But the southern seas are full of hazards, even greater than the perils of the Strait. Before the crews could celebrate their safe passage, a storm blew up with such violence that it sank the *Marigold* with all hands. Magellan had named the ocean *Pacific* – meaning peaceful – because he found it so calm, but the English sailors had never experienced waves so tall, or winds so strong. The *Elizabeth* and *Pelican* were blown back into the jaws of the Strait and their crews had to struggle for days against hurricane-force gusts driving them onto the rocks. Drake's ship managed to get out to sea, but John Wynter in the *Elizabeth* was swept further back into the channel, where he waited at anchor for Drake to return. After three weeks, with no sign of the other commander, Wynter gave the order to sail for home. He was imprisoned for desertion on Drake's return, though he always maintained that his crew would have mutinied if he'd asked them to brave entering the Pacific again.

Drake was left with only 80 men and his flagship, with a whole continent to plunder and an ocean 4,500 miles wide to sail across. Any sensible captain would have cancelled his mission. But the Dragon sailed north, preparing his ship for battle.

Drake's raiding got off to a bad start. On December 1, he stopped on the island of Mocha, off the coast of Chile, looking for fresh water and other supplies. But the Spanish invaders had already dubbed the region *tierra de guerra* – land of war – because the locals were fierce warriors. The *Pelican*'s landing party was attacked and four of her sailors slain. Drake himself was wounded twice in the head by arrows. He must have thought Doughty's ghost was having his revenge.

A few days later Drake's luck improved. The *Pelican* slipped into the port of Valparaiso and a raiding party boarded a Spanish merchant ship, *La Capitana*. Thinking the attackers were drunken local sailors, her crew laughed and offered them a barrel of wine. The last thing they were expecting was an English pirate attack and they carried no weapons. Drake would exploit this misplaced sense of security over the coming months.

The raiders took *La Capitana* and everything in her, including three chests of gold, valuable charts detailing the whole coast and hundreds of gallons of wine. The Dragon allowed himself a smile: once again he had a fighting fleet, and he'd struck gold too.

In a series of piratical raids that has never been equalled for daring or profit, the *Pelican* worked her way up the west coast of the Americas attacking ships and ports. Drake commandeered fishing boats, stole bullion from a caravan of llamas, and coins, emeralds and pearls from local merchants. On March 1, 1579, he chased and captured his greatest prize, a treasure ship carrying eighty pounds of Ecuadorian gold bars.

There was so much bullion on board, the Dragon replaced the stones that were used as ballast in the *Pelican*'s hold with silver ingots. He now had enough booty to begin plotting his journey home.

Drake called a meeting in his cabin with the pilots he had kidnapped from other ships. They advised him to sail west, across the mighty ocean and on to the Cape of Good Hope.

"You want me to sink in a Pacific storm," Drake cried. "That ocean is too dangerous to cross."

The pilots assured the captain that the route between Acapulco in Mexico and the Spice Islands in present-day Indonesia was indeed safe, but the best time to attempt it was in the winter months, when the trade winds were reliable. Drake scoffed at their suggestion, bragging that the *Pelican* would sail back to England through a secret northern passage, the Strait of Anian.

But this channel up in the polar seas was nothing more than a myth, popular among cartographers, and Drake had no intention of wasting his time searching for it. In truth, he was laying a smokescreen. When he released the captive pilots, they told the Spanish authorities the Dragon was sailing north, or perhaps bluffing and heading back to the Strait of Magellan. Drake calculated that any galleons sent from Spain would concentrate their search for him along the coast – while he would be sailing merrily across the Pacific. And he remembered the pilots' instructions. Drake anchored his ships in a quiet bay to make repairs, take on supplies and wait for the season to change.

The exact location of Drake's anchorage remains a mystery. Some historians believe that the *Pelican* sailed up as far as present-day San Francisco or Seattle, where the English sailors lived in a Native American village for six months. Others think the captain really did go searching for the fabled northwest passage, charting the unexplored coastline on a scrap of parchment – which has since vanished, of course. All we know for sure is that the *Pelican* arrived off Ternate in the Spice Islands, sometime around October, 1579. Drake and 60 of his men had survived the crossing.

Always with an eye out for a money-making scheme, Drake filled the last crevices of his ship's hold with a store of valuable local spices. Cloves, ginger and pepper were highly prized in Europe, and this cargo alone would have made Drake a rich man. He must have let out a sob when he was forced to throw most of it overboard in January 1580, to free his ship after she had run onto a reef.

It took ten weeks to cross the Indian Ocean, then a further month to reach Sierra Leone, on the west coast of Africa, where the crew stopped for fresh water. On September 26, they finally bobbed into Plymouth Bay and Drake hailed two fishermen in their boat.

"Is our Queen Elizabeth still alive?" he asked them in a hushed voice.

The bemused men nodded their heads and Drake

breathed a sigh of relief. He had been gone for almost three years and had no idea what his reception would be if a new monarch was on the throne. He was still cautious. Perhaps Spain and England were allies now, and his raids in the Pacific would be politically awkward. The crew moored the *Pelican* and Drake sent a rider to Elizabeth in London with a simple message: the Dragon had returned and his ship was full of gold.

Queen Elizabeth wasted no time in demonstrating her approval. Seven years after climbing the look-out tree in Panama, Francis Drake kneeled down on the dock at Greenwich, London, to be knighted by his queen. Elizabeth was rewarding him for his services to England – and the huge sums he had donated to the royal coffers. Drake had fulfilled his dreams. He was the first Englishman to sail around the world, and the first man to accomplish it in the same vessel. In later years he served as a politician and helped fight the Spanish Armada, before dysentery killed him in 1596, during a raid in the West Indies.

Pirate or patriot, soldier or thief, one thing is undisputed: Sir Francis Drake's epic voyage into the Pacific makes him one of history's greatest seafarers.

A Lighthouse Heroine

Longstone lighthouse, as it looks today

In the mist and spray thrown up by the storm, the survivors on the rock must have thought they were seeing things. A tiny rowing boat was nudging towards them out of the gloom, with a middle-aged man waving from its prow and a young girl pulling confidently at the oars. The girl's courage and proficiency startled the sailors in the party. They weren't used to seeing a woman who was as skilled on the water as they were. At any second, the sea threatened to pick the fragile craft up and smash it onto the same rocks that had crushed their own ship. But the girl worked the oars expertly, correcting the drift and turning into the waves to prevent the boat from capsizing. She rowed closer, never stopping to think of the danger she was in. Her name was Grace

Darling, and her daring at sea would make her one of the greatest celebrities of her times.

From crude fishing boats of sticks and animal hides to the vast warships of today, the history of Britain is in a large part the story of how its people have gone out on the sea. Before the age of flight, Britain relied on ships for trade and travel. The future of the country was decided by great naval battles and fortunes were made and lost on the ocean wave. Because of their close relationship to the sea, the British public was fascinated by nautical adventures. In the early 19th century, a story of the individual battling the might of the ocean reminded people of the struggles they faced in a time of overwhelming progress and change. Although sea adventures usually involve only a few individuals, they can sometimes have an effect on a whole nation.

Strange as it might seem, Grace's adventure began with the coming of the first British passenger ships. In 1838, long distance travel was a slow and bruising business. There were few good roads and the railway network hadn't been extended into the north of the country. The journey between Scotland and London, for example, took several days and nights in a cramped coach, bumping along rutted trails at the mercy of the weather. If passengers wanted any kind of luxury they were better off on the sea. With grand ballrooms, opulent bedrooms and a full social calendar, the new steamer ships were a forerunner of the great transatlantic liners and the age of first class, luxury travel.

The *Forfarshire* was a good example of this new style of passenger ship. She was powered by coal-fired boilers that turned two giant paddle wheels fixed to her hull. To give her additional speed on her route between Hull and Dundee, she was also rigged for sail – but her weight made wind alone an inadequate means of powering her, as her captain would soon discover. She had all the stately trimmings. There was china tableware at every meal and the saloon rooms were lavishly decorated with the works of a well-known artist. On the posters detailing her timetable, the ship was described as "splendid and powerful" by her owners.

With clouds of black smoke billowing from her funnel, the *Forfarshire* chugged out of Hull docks on September 6, 1838. By all accounts she was an impressive vessel. But this proud ship was no match for the fury of the sea.

The Northumbrian coastline north of Hull is a fearful stretch of churning seas and hidden reefs. Over the centuries, there have been more than 500 recorded wrecks in the area, and the cluster of 17 rocky outcrops that make up the Farne Islands is one of the most dangerous spots for shipping. As the *Forfarshire* approached these islands, her chief engineer rushed to the bridge. In a shocked voice, he reported to the captain that the boilers had flooded and could not be repaired until they reached a port.

The ship was suddenly powerless, except for her neglected sails. As if this wasn't bad enough, the captain noticed a knot of storm clouds rushing in from the west. By midnight, the *Forfarshire* was pitching and rolling on a huge sea that was driving her towards the rocky shore. One lifeboat got away from the ship, carrying a single passenger and eight sailors. The 52 people left on board could only stare and scream as the drifting ship smashed headlong into one of the islands - Big Harcar Rock.

The Farnes' reputation for wrecks had earned them a lighthouse, on Longstone Island. Its keepers - William and Thomasin Darling and their 22-year-old daughter, Grace - had listened to the pounding of the storm all night long, snug in their beds behind thick stone walls. In the dawn light of September 7, Grace and her father spotted the wreckage of a ship, grounded on an island almost a mile from the lighthouse. Grace could just make out a group of bedraggled survivors, clinging to the rocks.

According to reports published a few weeks later in the London press, Grace was woken in the night by the wailing cries of the castaways and went to rouse her father. But the storm that wrecked the *Forfarshire* raged for four whole days. The wind was blowing towards the mainland, carrying any cries away from the lighthouse. So, if Grace heard those desperate yells, she must have had the ears of a cat.

Father and daughter stared out across the swirling waters beyond the steps of their home. Could they save the castaways before they died of exposure or drowned? William Darling was an expert seaman and must have been wary of taking his small rowing boat out onto the storm-lashed waves to attempt a rescue. His son, William Jr., who also lived at the lighthouse was away with a fishing boat. So there was only Grace to aid him.

Some newspapers claimed Grace had to plead with her father to take his boat out, but this was disputed in other parts of the press. What is certain though, is that she helped William push the craft into the waves and jumped in alongside him, ready to risk her life to save the victims of the wreck.

For the first part of the crossing William rowed, but as they approached Big Harcar he let Grace take the oars. She brought the boat right to the edge of the island then kept it steady in the churning waters. Because it was impossible for them to make a landing without being broken on the rocks, William had to risk jumping ashore. He studied the crashing waves, waiting for the right moment, then took a great leap from the rocking prow and landed safely on the reef.

The boat was too small for everyone, so he quickly organized the survivors into two groups. There were nine of them in all: four crew and five passengers, one of whom was a Mrs. Dawson, still clutching the bodies of her two dead children. There was another corpse caught on the rocks – that of a minister who had died of exposure during the night. Some of the men had broken limbs and lacerations. All of them were trembling in the extreme cold. While this wretched party struggled to their feet, Grace held the boat in position on the wild sea.

At last, her father led Dawson and four of the men to the edge of the rocks and waited for his daughter to bring the boat as close as she dared. They managed to scramble in and Grace tended to their injuries while William and one of the sailors rowed back to the lighthouse. Grace and her mother led the survivors up the beach, leaving William and the strongest sailor to return for the other group.

An hour later, the castaways were huddled around the peat fire in the Darlings' living quarters, with Grace serving them hot drinks and fetching blankets. The lighthouse boat had saved nine lives – but at least 43 people had died.

For three days the bedraggled survivors lived with their rescuers, unable to leave the stone tower for fear of the storm. On the fourth day, the waters finally settled, and a fishing boat came over from the mainland to collect them. Within a few hours of their arrival, the first whispers were already spreading about the bravest girl on the seas – fearless Grace, the lighthouse heroine.

Up to the time of the rescue, the Darlings had led a simple – almost puritan – existence on Longstone. William was an enthusiastic gardener and ornithologist, from a long line of lighthousemen. His wife cooked the meals and worked at a spinning wheel by the fireside, while Grace, who had lived in a lighthouse since she was three weeks old, took care of the other domestic chores. She and her eight siblings had been home-schooled, with an emphasis on the stricter aspects of religion and morality. There were no playing cards in the lighthouse - *the Devil's books* was William's name for them - no novels, picture books or plays. For entertainment, Grace studied old maps or read Milton's weighty poetry. Perhaps she enjoyed the desolate beauty of the Farne Islands, the ever-changing seascape of mist, rocks and foaming water. But did a life encircled by the sea make her feel lonely? There can't have been too many gentlemen callers or visiting girlfriends out on Longstone. William Darling believed his daughter was safe from the evil temptations of the mainland: the dandies, novel readers and card players. Grace went back to work after the adventure in the rowing boat, like a princess dutifully returning to her tower.

But two weeks after the rescue, the first portrait artist arrived on the island with an easel slung over his shoulder. The celebrity photo-journalist of his day, this artist made a quick sketch of Grace and her father and sold it to a local newspaper. Reports of the Darlings' heroism had already started filtering out from remotest Northumbria. The London press sniffed a story and Grace's bravery - embellished by imaginative scribes - was a front page sensation. After the seventh portrait artist had come knocking on his door, William Darling grumbled in a letter to the press that the sittings were now over. He had been polite for long enough; the lighthouseman wanted all the fuss to die down.

Grace was receiving scores of letters from her admirers; people begged her for locks of her hair, or scraps of fabric from the dress she'd worn on the day of the rescue. She diligently replied to every inquiry, explaining in her careful handwriting that she was too busy with her chores ever to be lonely or bored on the island: "I have seven apartments in the house to keep in a state fit for gentlemen," she explained. It was impossible to send a keepsake of hair to everyone, Grace added, or in a few weeks' time she'd be wearing a wig. For Thomasin Darling it was all too much. She longed for the peace and quiet of Longstone to be restored. Her family wanted nothing to do with the realities of modern Britain, the march of progress, the big cities, factories and the masses of people who worked in them.

But the masses weren't finished with the Darlings.

Thomasin had good reason to fear the outside world and the changes that were taking place across Britain. In 1838, Dickens' *Oliver Twist* was published. His tale of poverty, crime and the workhouse was a stark commentary on the lives of millions of workers and the suffering they endured. Progress might have produced luxury steam boats like the *Forfarshire*, but it had also brought malnutrition, disease and dangerous working conditions for the common man, as the Industrial Revolution transformed the country. In a few years' time, growing public dissatisfaction would spark into political action and the workers would form unions, but for now they just wanted a distraction from their daily grind.

They craved entertainment, turning to the penny broadsheet newspapers for tales of adventure, catastrophe and heroism. If a story had all three elements – and the novelty of a heroine in the lead part – then all the better. But the press still felt obliged to offer moral instruction to their readers. Grace was the perfect role model. She was paraded in the press both as a daring adventuress and an example of Victorian womanhood at its best.

Grace had good company as a female icon for her times. Queen Victoria, who came to the throne in 1837, was a symbol of dutiful femininity in a troubled age, thought of as the mother of the nation. The Queen praised brave, heroic acts of course, but she also encouraged women to be content as humble homemakers. Grace was exciting, daring, even pretty, but she was also demure and respectable – an ideal Victorian heroine.

Throughout September and October, Grace-fever raged across the country. The letters came in a torrent, accompanied by visiting journalists, artists, circus owners – one begged Grace to sit in a lifeboat on the stage while his company performed – and all manner of cranks and admirers. Money came too. The Duke and Duchess of Northumberland were Grace *groupies*. They offered to set up a trust for her, banking all the donations and rewards that were arriving on Longstone. Queen Victoria herself sent a note for £50.

As well as money there were gold medals, commemorative watches and other gifts. Grace's portrait featured on hundreds of gaudy pottery designs and knick-knacks. Poets composed sonnets for her and the newspapers mentioned her by name when they wanted to point out an act of heroism. She even had to put up with a popular song that described the rescue, a schoolyard classic for years to come. This fascination with her name must have seemed intrusive and misplaced to the quiet girl and her family, who had been brought up on the waves. It was only when winter set in and their lighthouse was cut off from the mainland by heavy weather that the Darlings could relax.

Grace's fame had other disadvantages, aside from the loss of privacy. Fishermen along the coast scoffed at the idea that the Darlings had risked their lives during the rescue. They claimed that William and Grace were never in danger because they were always rowing in the lee - the sheltered side - of an island. So there was nothing heroic about it. Anyone who had grown up by the sea would have done the same, they argued.

Grace stayed silent throughout the unwanted press attention and the verbal attacks from within her own community. She knew that she'd been out in a storm strong enough to wreck a steamship, lee shore or not, but the backbiting must have hurt. Instead of spending more time on the mainland and enjoying her money and fame, Grace retreated into the private world of Longstone. The restless sea, that asked nothing of her, must have seemed like the company of a trusted friend.

But Grace couldn't hide on the lighthouse island forever. On a rare visit to the mainland, to visit her sister in the town of Bamburgh, she caught a chill. It was April 1842 and Grace was still exhausted by the pressures of unwanted celebrity. In her weakened condition, the cold worked its way into her chest and soon she was bedridden. Grace was racked with the disease that claimed so many of Britain's poor – tuberculosis. For months she faded away, until on October 20 she "went like snow" according to her sister, and died in her father's arms.

Grace Darling was buried in the grounds of Bamburgh Church and a memorial stone commemorating her life was planted out on the Farne Islands. One of England's best known poets, William Wordsworth, wrote some lines praising her bravery that were inscribed on her headstone. Her family wanted Grace to have a special monument in the churchyard, overlooking the sea, and this was completed in 1844. It features a stone statue of Grace reclining on a platform, an oar resting by her side.

Even in death, Grace couldn't escape the legend of her courage on the sea.

An Ultra-Secret Sinking

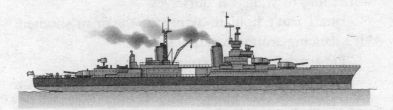

The unlucky cruiser, *USS Indianapolis*

Lieutenant Wilbur Gwinn was cursing his bad luck. Before he'd left base that morning his flight commander had asked him to test a new kind of navigational aerial. It was a thick wire, trailed from the rear of the Ventura bomber that Gwinn captained. But the weight that held the aerial in place after take-off had snapped free. Gwinn returned to base to collect a new one, but this had broken too and the aerial was flailing about so much he couldn't get a proper signal. One of his gunners was fixing it, but he was taking too long for Gwinn's liking. They were cruising 650km (400 miles) out over the Pacific and Gwinn wanted to get on with his real mission – to hunt for Japanese submarines and, if possible, to blow them out of the water. It was July 1945, the last, desperate days of the Second World War.

"Take the wheel while I sort this thing out," Gwinn grumbled to his copilot. He hurried along the fuselage tunnel of the bomber to the rear of the plane, where the gunner was stretched out by a hatch in the floor.

"Pull that thing in," Gwinn growled. "We'll find something to weight it ourselves."

"But I can't hold it, skipper," the man shouted. "It's dancing around too much."

"Let me have a try," replied Gwinn.

The pilot got down on his front and stretched an arm through the hatch. The biting cold of the outside air startled him and he stared down at the ocean for a moment, trying to catch his breath.

"What is it, skipper?" the gunner cried. His captain had suddenly pulled himself up from the floor and was racing back towards the cockpit. "Look at the water," Gwinn called over his shoulder.

The gunner crouched over and studied the ocean. He squinted and saw a thin line, like a river snaking across a plain. It was an oil slick, the kind left by a submarine running on the surface.

Gwinn sounded battle stations and brought his plane down so low it was almost skimming over the waves. Flying at maximum speed, and with its guns and depth charges primed, the bomber followed the twisting stain towards the horizon. Any second, Gwinn expected to see the shape of a submarine conning tower slicing through the ocean swell. But what he found was completely unexpected. Gwinn saw men. From his cruising height of 3,000 feet, they had been invisible against the shimmering sea. But at low altitude, he could spot them easily. A few were in US Navy rafts, but most bobbed helplessly in the water in their lifejackets. They were stretched out for miles across the ocean, clustered in small groups. There were other shapes down there among them, menacing shadows flitting beneath the surface. Sharks circled the swimmers, at times rushing in to strike.

"Get that radio working," Gwinn cried. "We've got sailors in the water. Hundreds of them. Something big must have gone down."

Gwinn had stumbled across the survivors of the US Navy's worst disaster at sea – the sinking of the *USS Indianapolis*. These men had already been in the water for three days and nights when they saw the bomber swoop down out of the sky. If Gwinn hadn't chanced across them, they would almost certainly have all died. There were no rescuers looking for them, no search planes or patrol ships in the area. The crew of the *Indianapolis* had been on an assignment so secret, nobody even knew they were missing.

Since her launch in November, 1931, the heavy cruiser *USS Indianapolis* had been one of the most valued ships in the American fleet. She could make a breathtaking speed of 32 knots and her equipment and fittings were considered state of the art. When navy chiefs were asked to provide a fast ship for a mission that might influence the entire outcome of the war, *USS Indianapolis* was an obvious choice.

In early July 1945, the ship had been at anchor in the Mare Island Naval Yard in Southern California.

She had been undergoing repairs following a *kamikaze* attack that killed 13 crewmen during the battle for Okinawa, a fortified island in the East China Sea. On the morning of July 16, the ship's captain, Charles Butler McVay, received orders to transport a special cargo to the Western Pacific airbase of Tinian, via Hawaii. He watched from the deck as a mysterious wooden crate was loaded on board. It was escorted by a detachment of elite guards who remained on the ship, acting as guards. If that wasn't enough of a riddle for the *Indianapolis'* 1,196 crew, a globe of solid lead was carried up to the captain's quarters and bolted to the steel plates of the deck. McVay didn't know what was inside this peculiar container. He was simply ordered to deliver it to the other side of the world, and at maximum speed.

Perhaps it was just as well that McVay had been kept in the dark about his cargo. Inside the lead sphere was one of the deadliest substances on Earth: uranium-235. The *Indianapolis* was carrying the makings of an atomic bomb.

In the spring of 1945, the war was all but over - except for the last struggles of the Japanese military, who refused to accept defeat. Allied commanders decided that a massive show of force might persuade them to abandon their historic tradition of choosing death before surrender. The grim task of clearing every enemy-held island in the Pacific was costing the lives of thousands of American Marines. Perhaps the annihilation of a major Japanese city would demonstrate how futile it was to continue fighting? In the deserts of New Mexico, a team of physicists set about developing the atom bomb.

By July they had tested a prototype and had the parts ready for two bombs. Because these devices were so unstable, the scientists advised against flying them to the base where they would be assembled. An ocean crossing was the safest option, but it would have to be a speedy ship. Every day of war brought more Allied casualties.

Captain McVay was a respected Navy man and destined for the highest ranks. He had already won a silver star for gallantry, and his bravery was matched by his seamanship: he knew how to get the best out of his ship and crew. The *Indianapolis* broke speed records en route to Hawaii, completing the voyage in only seventy-four and a half hours. Taking just six hours to resupply, the cruiser left for the US-controlled island of Tinian, 3,300 miles to the southwest. She arrived there on July 26, 1945 and her apocalyptic cargo was handed over to the US Airforce.

The mission had been a success. The *Indianapolis* should have finished the war in glory, after years of exemplary service. Instead, because of a tragic breakdown in communications she was torn apart and destroyed only four days later, almost on the eve of peace.

The ship proceeded to the small island of Guam, just south of Tinian, where Captain McVay received new orders to cross the Philippine Sea to the naval

An Ultra-Secret Sinking

base over a thousand miles away at Leyte. He was to report to Admiral McCormick on the battleship *Idaho*. McVay and his officers made all the proper checks for the voyage to Leyte – along a busy shipping lane known as Route Peddie. As they were told there was no particular hazard or submarine threat in the area, the *Indianapolis* wasn't offered a destroyer escort, even though there was no SONAR equipment on board. She left port on July 28, due to dock in Leyte early on July 31.

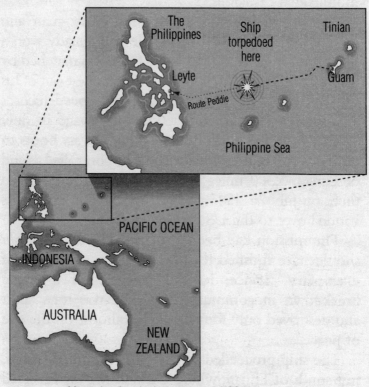

Maps showing the last voyage of *USS Indianapolis*

It was the last time she would put to sea. Captain McVay had been tragically misinformed.

Three days before the *Indianapolis* docked in Guam, the destroyer *USS Underhill* had been escorting a convoy of freighters, close to Route Peddie. One of her lookouts spotted a submarine's periscope breaking the waves and the *Underhill's* captain gave the order to ram. Seconds later, the ship was blown apart by an ear-splitting explosion. She had inadvertently rammed a Kaiten - a *kamikaze* torpedo released by a Japanese submarine. These deadly tubes were 48 feet long and carried a human suicide pilot. One hundred and nineteen American sailors died as a result of the blast.

There was a predator stalking Route Peddie, a fully-equipped enemy sub. Naval intelligence knew this before the *Indianapolis* left Guam but, due to a security misunderstanding, Captain McVay wasn't notified. The coded messages that described the sinking of the *Underhill* were classified Ultra-Secret. This level of security was so tight, it wasn't even shown to the staff who could have warned McVay.

Suspended just below the ocean surface in his submarine *I-58*, Commander Mochitsura Hashimoto watched the shipping lane for his next victim.

Just after midnight on July 30, a torpedo hammered into the starboard hull of the *Indianapolis*, ripping away the bow in an explosion of flame. A second torpedo tore into her, below the bridge tower. It was a simple strike for Hashimoto, out in the heart of the Philippine Sea. Through his periscope he saw a great fireball shoot up from the silhouette of the cruiser. Congratulating his officers on a job well done, he ordered his sub down into the quiet depths.

The huge battleship tore through the waves at her cruising speed of 17 knots, scooping up water through the 40 foot gaping hole where her prow had once been. In the 12 minutes it took for her to sink, she kept pushing forwards through the water, hastening her own end. Every electrical connection in the ship had been disabled by the second explosion and there was no way for the officers on the bridge to contact the engine room to order a propeller shutdown. Although there was no damage to the aft sections of the ship, she was taking so much water she was doomed. The *Indianapolis* began to list, steadily corkscrewing into the waves. Eight minutes after the first torpedo detonated, McVay gave the hardest order any captain could give: *Abandon Ship*.

Amid all the chaos and destruction, there was still some smattering of good luck. Midnight was the change of watch for the crew, so most of the sailors were awake and fully clothed when the torpedoes hit. Many of them had enough time to find a lifejacket and scramble up to the open air. Hundreds of men lined up on the tilting deck, waiting until the angle of list was so steep they could simply step into the water. They were left bobbing in small groups in the ship's wake, strung out across the ocean for miles.

Around 300 crewmen lost their lives inside the *Indianapolis*, in the torpedo explosions, the fires that swept through her cramped corridors beneath decks and in the walls of water that surged in from her broken bow. An estimated 900 men went into the water alive. Among them were sailors badly-burned, others suffering from shock, or bleeding and choking in the thousands of gallons of fuel oil that clogged the sea from the cruiser's punctured tanks. These men spent that first night trying to stay alive until the morning, sure that their rescuers would arrive with the dawn.

But the castaways were only at the beginning of their ordeal.

The survivors watched the sun rise on July 30 and every man must have wondered: "How long will it be before they come for us?" They didn't know that because of the electrical blackout, the ship's radio operators had failed to send an SOS. The only message that was picked up by Naval Intelligence coming from that area was sent by a Japanese submarine. Her captain was reporting a successful attack on a large battleship. The message was decoded but ignored. Enemy subs were notorious for their false claims and trickery. At the beginning of the war the US Navy might have taken notice, but they had been deceived too often by false reports. Hashimoto's message was tossed aside.

The sailors in the water passed the hours trying to

organize themselves into groups, checking their supplies and nursing the injured. Captain McVay was in a cluster of three rafts with about ten other men. He estimated that only 30 or 40 sailors could have survived the sinking. The captain had no idea that the majority of his crew was floating around him, dispersed across miles of open water. The groups varied in size; the largest cluster on the sea contained over 400 men. This mass of injured and frightened sailors had no rafts or supply stocks between them. They bobbed in a great mass of lifejackets, splashing arms and heads. In the first few hours after the ship went down, 50 of them died from their injuries. Some of them were unconscious, tied to the group by ropes or supported by friends. Lieutenant Haynes, one of the ship's doctors, tested to see if a sailor was still alive by touching one of his pupils. If the man didn't react to this stimulus, his lifejacket was removed and he slipped away.

That afternoon two spotter planes flew overhead but, like Gwinn on his patrol, they were too high up to notice the men in the water. All efforts to attract their attention with mirrors, shouts or flares came to nothing. The men consoled themselves with the fact that they were due in Leyte the next morning and would be missed.

No rescuers came that first day. But the sharks did. In the late afternoon their silvery bodies started weaving between the groups. They moved slowly through the water, dropping away into the blue gloom when a sailor splashed his hand in the water or yelled for help. Soon, they would not be so timid.

By the end of their second day in the water the survivors were beginning to feel the strain. Being stranded on the open sea can make a man feel overwhelmed and helpless. Trapped between two great expanses of blue, the pitiless sea and the endless canopy of the sky, some of the sailors started to panic. Discipline crumbled as they fought with each other over water supplies, a space on a raft, even a better lifejacket. Burned by the tropical sun, crazed by thirst, some of the men started drinking saltwater. These were the first to go insane.

As the night wore on, the sailors couldn't understand why they hadn't been saved. The planes that had droned past were all on bombing missions or routine patrols. There was no reason for them to be looking for castaways. But where were the search ships, the planes scouring the waves? There were none, because nobody was looking for the *Indianapolis*. In a terrible twist of bad luck, the radio signal sent from Guam to the *USS Idaho*, describing the route of the ship, had been lost or ignored. To make matters worse, there was a standing order at Leyte Naval Base prohibiting the report of arriving battleships. Enemy spies might be able to use the information. But this order was interpreted as meaning that nonarrival shouldn't be reported either.

The naval authorities who had been expecting the cruiser assumed she had been ordered to another corner of the world's oceans. Caught in a tangle of ultra-secret orders and procedural confusion, the

Indianapolis disappeared from naval positioning charts. There were no rescue ships, because there was no rescue.

On the third day, the sharks grew bolder. The exhausted men watched as one darted in, nosing towards their group. At a given signal the sailors would kick the water, shout and wave their arms. Sometimes the silent predator would turn away and begin circling the group again. There were other times when no amount of noise or splashing would deter the attacker. He sighted his victim and rolled in beneath the terrified man, snapping and gnawing until his teeth had caught hold, then yanking his body away from the outstretched arms of his friends, dragging him down to the underwater shadows.

Scores of men were taken by sharks. The sailors closed ranks, linked arms and tried to fight off the killers. But all too often these attempts were useless.

This was only one of the horrors the men had to face. By now, their hunger and thirst was so terrible they began to hallucinate. A crazed sailor announced that he had discovered a current of fresh water, rippling ten feet below the surface. He dived and came up a minute later, smiling, describing the taste of cool, pure water on his cracked lips. He was drinking the sea, of course, and hours later he would be in a coma or dead. But the torment of his friends was unending.

Other men claimed they could see the wrecked ship on the seabed below them. They said it was possible to swim down to the drinking fountains stationed along the decks and take a refreshing sip. When a feeble sailor broke away from the group to investigate, he was taken immediately by a prowling shark.

A party of men even decided they could swim to the Philippines and raise the alarm. They floated around the scattered groups recruiting their friends for the 500 mile journey. Despite the desperate pleas of their officers, they set off at dusk, swimming into oblivion. None of this group was seen alive again.

It was a nightmare in the water for the castaways. As darkness fell, they listened in agony to the screams of their crewmates, the thrashings of the sharks and the mutterings of the insane. Those men who still had their wits about them wondered how they could endure another night. When the light came they scanned the empty sky, knowing this day would be their last chance of salvation.

Gwinn's bomber droned over the horizon at 11:25 in the morning – the rescue operation had finally begun.

Lieutenant Gwinn estimated there were 150 men in the water, scattered over 20 square miles of ocean. He dropped his emergency rafts, some food and water canisters and then circled overhead, sending frantic radio messages back to base. When his commander heard the reports, he contacted all the naval ships in the Philippine Sea. But the nearest vessel was more than a hundred miles away from the survivors. The men would have to wait another 12 hours before the Navy got there. Meanwhile, Gwinn's plane was running short of fuel. Reluctant to abandon the sailors, the airforce sent a seaplane captained by Lieutenant Adrian Marks. His orders were to patrol the area and drop supplies if possible. But when Marks saw the shark carnage below him, he decided to make a landing. In a feat of amazing courage, Marks slammed his lumbering Catalina Seaplane into the waves and managed to keep her upright. With his copilot leaning out of a side door, Marks taxied across the sea, picking up survivors. By the time the first rescue ship arrived, Marks had over fifty ragged sailors crammed into his plane and spread across the wings. But it was already midnight, and the ship had to wait for dawn before she could begin a proper search.

On August 3, 1945, the survivors of *USS Indianapolis* were at last rescued from their trial in the water. There were 316 sailors who were plucked from the sea. Over 500 men had made it off the ship alive, only to perish in the water.

The sinking of the *Indianapolis* was a terrible blow for the US Navy. Captain McVay – in the last group of men to be rescued – was held responsible for the disaster. Following a bizarre court martial, where one of the key witnesses against him was Captain Hashimoto, McVay was reprimanded for not plotting a zig-zag course. This tactic was sometimes used as an anti-submarine measure, but McVay had decided not to adopt it, because he had no reason to think there were any subs in the area. And, besides, zigzagging was ineffective against a skilled submarine crew.

McVay was demoted and his career ruined. The captain never recovered from the disgrace of being blamed for the loss of his ship and so many of his crew. He killed himself with his service revolver in November 1968.

But his death wasn't the end of the *Indianapolis* affair. In 1996, a Florida teenager, Hunter Scott, began writing a school history project on the ship's sinking. His curiosity had been roused after he saw the movie *Jaws*, which includes a scene describing the nightmare the *Indianapolis* crewmen had lived through. Scott contacted some of the survivors and asked them about their experiences. Every one of them praised their captain and criticized the findings of his court martial. A determined young man, Scott decided to help clear McVay's name by taking the case to his representative congressman in Washington. In October 2000, after an energetic campaign, Captain McVay was exonerated for the loss of his ship.

It was a closing act of decency, in the tragic loss of a ship and three-quarters of her crew.

Cape Crusader

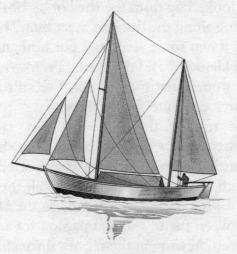

Legh II, under sail

In 1934, an Argentinian cattle-rancher and amateur yachtsman, Vito Dumas, was building a boat to take him around the world. *Legh II* was 9.5m (31 feet) long and 3m (10 feet) wide, with a pointed prow and stern. She had a massive underwater keel - 3,500kg (7,700 lbs) of cast-iron - to keep her upright in the heaviest seas. This shape of ship is known as Norwegian: fishermen from Norway have perfected the design over hundreds of years, testing it on the storm-lashed polar waters where they make their living. Dumas had good reason to seek inspiration from these hard-bitten mariners: his boat had to be able to withstand waves bigger than houses and winds that could uproot trees. As part of his circumnavigation he planned to sail around Cape Horn – alone. It had never been done before.

Dumas looked up from the shell of his boat. A man was hurrying along the dock to meet him. The visitor scampered down some steps and put his hand out.

"I'm Al Hansen," said the man. "From what I hear we've got something in common. I've sailed solo to Buenos Aires, en route for the Horn."

For the rest of that day the two yachtsmen discussed their tactics, their hopes and the ships they were entrusting with their lives. They parted as firm friends, with Dumas wishing Hansen all the luck in the world for his voyage. The assault on the Horn was a bond between them, a shared passion for adventure that had been brewing in them both since childhood. Only five men had made a solo circumnavigation before then, and none had dared face the Cape.

Both Hansen and Dumas would go on to challenge that desolate crag of ice and rock in the Southern Ocean. Hansen was the first solo-sailor to make it around the Cape – sailing from East to West. But it was a cruel victory. His splintered craft – *Mary Rose* – was dragged out of the surf along the coast of Chile only a few weeks after he'd chatted with Dumas in the boatyard. Cape Horn demanded a terrible penalty from anyone reckless enough to sail into its waters. Hansen's ship had broken apart only a few miles after passing the Horn, and his body was never recovered.

Dumas was appalled by the loss of his new friend. As *Legh II* slowly took shape he wondered if the dream of beating the Cape was worth the risk. As his resolve crumbled, so did his settled life in Argentina. Dumas was a rancher and exporter. His business started to fail as the world edged towards war and European countries cancelled their international orders. At the same time, his marriage fell apart too. In the end, he was forced to sell his beloved new ship to buy a tractor, swapping a craft that skims the waves for one to furrow the earth.

It would be eight long years before he got *Legh II* back, and set off on his extraordinary voyage.

Like so many drawn to the sea, Dumas' childhood was far from privileged. Born in Buenos Aires, Argentina, in 1900, he left school at 14 when his father's tailoring business faltered. Working as a brass-polisher and errand boy, Dumas used the few pesos he earned to help put food on the table. Despite the taunts of his old schoolmates, he never complained about his lot. Instead, he accepted the ups and downs of life and enjoyed his free time to the full. He grew into an outgoing and talented young man, excelling at sports, painting and singing. With a barrel-chested physique and boundless energy, he relished setting himself seemingly impossible challenges.

When he was 19, Dumas announced to his friends that he would swim the River Plate - the world's widest river - which runs between Argentina and Uruguay. At the age of 23, he crossed the 26 miles of churning tides in twenty-five hours. In 1931, he abandoned an attempt to swim the English Channel and set off instead for Argentina from Arcachon, in southwest France, sailing a yacht only 26 feet long, *Legh*. (This peculiar name was taken from the jumbled-up initials of Dumas' girlfriend.) It was a characteristically reckless adventure. Many of his sailing friends said he was crazy even to attempt the voyage in such a small craft. After 74 days at sea, a beaming Dumas docked in Buenos Aires and read his name in the newspaper headlines. He adored the media attention. Riding on this wave of fame, Dumas commissioned *Legh II* and prepared for the circumnavigation of the world. Then came the visitor to the dry dock, and the spell of bad luck that would delay his departure for so many years.

When his business failed, Dumas found work on a cattle ranch, out on the pampas. As the seasons slipped by, he tried to ignore the lure of the sea. But his dreams still haunted him. He found himself sniffing the breeze for the scent of the faraway ocean. On rainy days, he pored over old charts, endlessly plotting a lonely voyage around the globe, aiming for Cape Horn from the West. Hansen had already proved that the route from the East was possible – but it had cost him his life. Prevailing winds made that course easier than the western approach. Dumas wasn't even sure if his route was possible, but at the age of 41 he realized that if he didn't make the attempt soon he would regret it for the rest of his life.

In true Dumas style, it seemed the worst possible time to depart. It was 1942 and the Second World

War was raging. The seas were full of gunboats and prowling submarines. His friends told him he would be blown out of the water.

"But I will sail in the empty Southern Ocean," Dumas replied, "through the latitude of the *roaring forties*, where other ships fear to sail because of high winds and storms. And if I don't carry a radio, nobody will mistake me for a spy. Argentina is a neutral country, so I have nothing to fear."

"It's a good thing you don't plan to take a radio," said one man. "How could you afford one, Vito? You don't have a peso to your name."

"I will borrow what I need," Dumas replied confidently. "My friends have always been generous. They will help to provision my boat."

"What boat?" cried another man. "Have you forgotten, you sold *Legh II*?"

But Dumas was right to trust the generosity of his friends. They understood how important the voyage was to him. He was sailing to prove his own courage, and to show that even in the grip of world war there was still a place for noble gestures. The solo voyage was a quest to remind people what great things they were capable of, away from the crushing forces of destruction, fighting and fear.

A friend gave Dumas the money he needed to buy back *Legh II*. The workers around the docks in Buenos Aires heard about the voyage; they offered their spare time and skills for free, joining together to make the ship seaworthy. People all over the city sent offerings: hand-knitted socks, torn overcoats, bottles of wine and cans of food donated one or two at a time. Another friend asked Dumas how much cash he was taking with him. He was startled when the budding circumnavigator revealed that his wallet held only a few pesos. The friend gave him ten English pounds – *Legh II's* total kitty. In only a few weeks, Dumas had everything he needed.

By the day of his departure, the whole country was taking an interest in the madcap venture around the world's oceans. Dumas left Buenos Aires on June 27, 1942, with a huge crowd cheering him off on the first leg of his journey. He was heading for Cape Town, South Africa, then on to Wellington, New

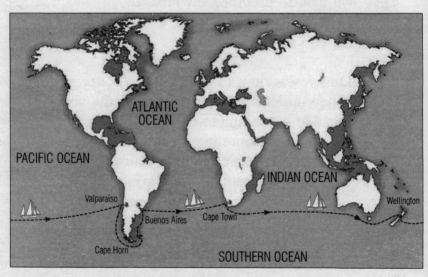

Map showing Vito Dumas' route around the world

Zealand and finally Valparaiso in Chile, before his final, lonely battle against the Horn.

The first week of sailing was a brutal reminder of the might of the sea. *Legh II* ran straight into a *pampero* – a violent squall of high winds and hammering waves. Dumas couldn't leave the tiller for several days, in case the boat turned sideways on to a wave and was capsized. He tore his hands changing the rigging, and was thrown about all over the deck. True to their nickname, the winds at 40° were relentless and strong, gusting at 50 knots. By July 5, Dumas' body was showing the strain. His cuts grew infected and his right arm began to swell, until it was as thick as his thigh. Sailing away from South America, into a band of sea that no solo yachtsman had dared enter before, Dumas wondered if he'd finally bitten off more than he could chew.

By July 10, the arm was foul-smelling and useless. He could no longer work the tiller or manage the sails properly. After securing the boat as best he could, he went down to the cabin and lay on his bunk. He had a grim task ahead of him. If the arm continued to fester, he would die of blood poisoning. At dawn he would have to amputate the infected limb. He closed his eyes, said a prayer, then tried to rest.

He woke to find himself soaked in putrid liquid: during the night his arm had burst open and disgorged the poisoned blood. It wasn't a pretty sight, but Dumas knew that the limb was saved. He tended it for a day or two, thanked whoever had answered his prayer and went back to the tiller.

Gradually his body hardened to the demands of solo sailing. In the roaring forties the winds were rarely less than gale-force, but Dumas learned how to set the sails so his ship cut through the tallest waves and held up well. His cheeriness never failed him. He took great joy in preparing simple meals of soup and hot chocolate, watching the ever-changing seascape and singing to himself, so he could hear the sound of a human voice.

On August 31, after 55 days at sea and 6,700km (4,200 miles), Dumas sighted the great ridge of Cape Town's Table Mountain looming on the horizon. By midnight, *Legh II* was moored safely in the docks and Dumas was drinking rum with an excited group of sailors and bemused locals. The first leg of his journey was behind him.

For three weeks, Dumas was toasted and cheered in the yachting clubs of Cape Town. In sailing circles his achievement made him a celebrity, but the oddball Argentinian was a welcome diversion from the hardships of war even for landlubbers. In his usual way, Dumas instantly made friends and took any help that was offered. He even accepted groceries and navigation charts from generous shopkeepers. But, although he enjoyed his fame, he was anxious to get back to sea. The biggest challenges lay ahead.

On September 14, he was escorted from Cape Town by a flotilla of small yachts. *Legh II* was heading into the most desolate reaches of the Indian Ocean, bound for Wellington, a mammoth voyage 12,000km (7,400 miles) to the East.

Dumas sailed straight into the worst storm he'd ever encountered. Again, he stayed at the tiller, trying to keep the boat running head on into the waves. Unlike later solo yachtsmen, Dumas had no self-steering mechanism. His was a shoestring operation and he scorned gadgetry – he sailed with only one screwdriver and didn't even bother to carry a bilge pump. When he needed to bail water he used a bucket. He was an old-school sailor, staying at the helm for as long as he could, then darting down below to catch a few hours of sleep when the winds permitted.

The crashing waves weren't the only danger. One morning, Dumas saw three waterspouts – mini-tornadoes – rushing towards him. The wind was sucking up the wave-tops into funnels of swirling foam that could rip the masts off a small boat. He had to swing the tiller desperately to steer safely around them.

Whales were another hazard. Although Dumas was a nature lover – he wouldn't even kill a fish during his voyage – he watched in horror as the huge mammals nuzzled up to his boat. One sweep of their tails could have capsized her.

But, despite the constant gales and the forty-foot waves, Dumas still found plenty to lift his spirits. He made friends with a Cape pigeon, throwing him bits of food until the bird was comfortable enough in his company to ride along on the deck. Another companion was a humble fly that Dumas came across one day in the cabin. He fostered the insect, feeding it sugar and letting it crawl around on his hand. The months at sea had made everything associated with dry land fascinating to him and he marvelled at the ability of animals to adapt to their habitat.

But the hard work around the boat was taking its toll. The storms were unrelenting, his body was covered in cuts and bruises and when his gums started aching he realized that he was falling victim to the sailor's disease: *scurvy*. But Dumas refused to change course and head north where he might find a safe port in Australia. He pressed on doggedly for New Zealand.

On December 27, after 104 days alone on the waves, he entered Wellington's docks and breathed a sigh of relief.

Dumas rested in port, letting his body heal and tending to his battered ship. To speed the repairs, he enlisted the help of some Allied sailors, paying them in Scotch whisky – another kind donation from his supporters in Buenos Aires. Once again he made new friends and was celebrated for his daring journey across the roaring forties. Then he set out to sea again on January 30, 1943, creeping back towards his own continent.

The voyage across the Pacific was tranquil and Dumas was able to relax a little. He spent more time sleeping, cooking and watching the whales and birds that accompanied *Legh II*. On April 11, the ship was bobbing off the port of Valparaiso in Chile. He had crossed his third ocean – a stretch of 8,000km (5,000 miles) of open water.

There was no wind for the sails, so Dumas hailed a passing fishing boat and asked them for a tow. The crew was startled when they discovered who the lone sailor was – his story was in all the South American newspapers. They took him to a safe dock and gave Dumas a welcome party that lasted well into the next day.

Only Cape Horn lay ahead of him now: the greatest challenge of all. Dumas prepared his ship and his nerves for the ordeal, while his hosts in Valparaiso urged caution. They argued that since he had already achieved so much, why risk everything at the last hurdle. But Dumas had been planning his battle with the Horn for ten years, studying the maps and the weather systems, working out the optimum dates and routes for success. He knew that he had to beat the Cape or the whole voyage would have been for nothing. On May 25 he set sail for home, another 5,000km (3,200 miles) away, via the Horn.

It was almost as though the Cape knew he was coming. Approaching the tip of the continent, the temperature dropped sharply and the winds began to howl in *Legh II's* rigging. A fine mist shrouded the ship and it was hard for Dumas to sight land, even though he was only a few miles off the coast. By June 10, giant waves were breaking over the deck. It was so cold Dumas had to light matches under his fingers to restore the sensation in his hands. It took up to ten seconds before he could feel his skin burning. But Dumas wouldn't turn back: he sailed right past the opening of the Strait of Magellan without being tempted to take this easier passage through to the Atlantic. He was on a mission and, despite the worsening conditions, he continued steering for the south.

Gradually the sinister mood of the Cape began to corrode Dumas' confidence. Staring into the icy waves that hammered into his ship he started thinking of Hansen and all the other drowned sailors who rested on the sea floor below him. Perhaps he was wrong to challenge the power of nature? Was he mocking Cape Horn, and risking its wrath?

As he neared the latitude of the Horn the seas grew fiercer. Trying to snatch a moment's rest from the frozen tiller, Dumas went down to the cabin. He was standing in darkness when a wave rocked the boat so violently he was thrown into the planks head first. Dumas screamed in pain then examined his bloody face. His nose was broken and he had cuts in his mouth and across his cheeks. It took him half an hour to steady himself and bandage his wounds. When he was finished he realized that in the time that had elapsed he must have rounded the Cape. He'd triumphed. The cost of a broken nose was nothing to what others had sacrificed.

Dumas struggled up the coast of Argentina, fighting gales and barely able to eat because of the wounds in his mouth. He was in constant pain and the seas were still raging – but he was jubilant. His battle in the roaring forties was over. He was the first man to round the cape from the West. If only he could get back to Buenos Aires alive, he would have beaten Cape Horn and lived to tell the tale.

On July 7, 1943, Vito Dumas approached Mar del Plata, a port just to the south of Buenos Aires. His homecoming prompted national celebrations and earned him a commendation from the Argentinian government. Great crowds streamed down to the Buenos Aires docks two months later, when *Legh II* anchored for an official welcoming ceremony. Yachtsmen the world over saluted Dumas' bravery. In just under thirteen months he had sailed 33,000km (20,400 miles), the majority of them through the roaring forties – which had always been a virtual no-go area for solo yachtsmen.

Dumas went on to make several more voyages and established himself as one of the world's greatest sailors. In 1957, he was awarded the first Slocum Prize, the ultimate mark of respect for solo navigators. He continued to paint, write and explore the world's oceans until his death in 1965.

The Galley Slaves

The rowing boat, *Britannia II*, and her crew

It was a small white tip shark, no more than four feet long. Only a baby really. John Fairfax didn't pay him much attention. He was too busy chasing a school of fish, trying to speargun a few for dinner. As long as the shark kept its distance, there'd be no trouble. But the white tip had his own ideas about who was the strongest predator underwater. Each time he circled the school, he swung in a little closer. Eventually, Fairfax had to tap him on the nose with a spear to drive him away. It was still no more than an irritation. When he'd lived in the Caribbean, Fairfax had killed sharks twice as big with only his diving knife. On his row across the Atlantic three years earlier, he'd fought off an attacking 12 foot mako, the deadliest species of shark after the great white. On this voyage, rowing across the Pacific with his girlfriend, Sylvia Cook, Fairfax had been swimming for months with white tips, brown sharks and other killers that shadowed the boat. Fairfax saw no cause for alarm.

He shot a small fish and was diving to collect it when the white tip surged forward and swallowed his catch whole. That was taking things too far. Fairfax shot the white tip through the head with one of his spears. But the shaft didn't have a barb to hold it in place; it flashed right through and the shark twitched, turned and went for him.

They grappled underwater for a few minutes, until Fairfax had his thrashing opponent in a firm grip. He started back-paddling through the waves, pulling the shark towards the boat. When he reached its side, he shouted to Sylvia to pass him a gutting knife. Fairfax wanted revenge. No scavenger of a shark was going to pinch his dinner. He caught the knife from Sylvia and slit the shark's belly open, in a reckless act of anger and pride.

The shark, bleeding to death, twisted free and clamped its jaws around Fairfax's upper right arm. With his shoulder burning in pain Fairfax forced his fingers into the shark's gills to shove it away. His attacker dragged him a few yards then dived, leaving a plume of blood like red mist in the water. Fairfax gulped for air on the surface, tried to cover the wound with his left hand and splashed towards the boat, leaving his own scarlet wake behind him.

Sylvia watched his approach. She thought he must be hugging a fish to his chest, because of his awkward swimming style. It was only when he flopped over the side that she saw the hole in his arm.

"Make me a tourniquet," he asked her, trying to keep his voice calm.

While Cook quickly knotted a handkerchief around his arm, Fairfax dragged himself up so he was propped against the bulwarks, trying to slow his racing heart. He knew he had to help his body deal with the trauma of the attack, the loss of tissue and blood. Already, the skin on his face was waxen and his eyes had lost their usual sparkle. As soon as he could think straight, he turned to examine his shoulder. It looked as though his whole upper arm had burst open. He glanced up at Sylvia and her face said it all. They were thousands of miles out in the Pacific, the radio transmitter hadn't worked for weeks and it was hurricane season. Now he was shark-bitten - and badly.

"Get the camera," he said. "This is going to make a great picture."

John Fairfax had always lived a dangerous life: he once described himself as a professional adventurer. Growing up in South America, he'd explored the Amazon's forests while working as a trapper, driven across the USA in a sports car and partied with Panamanian pirates - all before he was out of his twenties. He believed in setting himself challenges, testing himself to the limits of mental and physical endurance. It was no surprise when he was finally drawn to the ocean, the great arena for so many would-be heroes.

In 1966 he was living in London, making preparations to row across the Atlantic. Fairfax dismissed sailing as the easy option; he wanted to do something people thought impossible, something Herculean. As a teenager he'd been fascinated by the story of George Harbo and Frank Samuelson, two Norwegians who'd grown bored of their jobs as clam diggers in 19th century New Jersey and decided to make their names as the first men to row an ocean. They completed the Atlantic West to East crossing in 1896, taking 55 days and 13 hours in an 18 foot open boat – the *Fox*. Their time has never been bettered.

Fairfax admired the two men for taking on the ocean and daring to believe they could succeed. He wanted to do something similarly groundbreaking and, as he'd been a loner all his life, the idea of a solo crossing appealed to him. It would be a world first if he could pull it off.

But there were two major obstacles: he had little rowing experience and even less cash. Ignoring these difficulties with his usual bravado, Fairfax started a daily exercise routine that included hours of uninterrupted rowing around the Serpentine in Hyde Park, in London. But the Serpentine is little more than a large pond, a far cry from the ocean that covers 20% of the Earth's surface and is teeming with whales, killer sharks and icebergs. As the weeks turned to months, Fairfax was still struggling up and down in his boat, and he gained invaluable experience coping with the tedium of long-distance rowing. His training might have seemed eccentric, but it was also effective. He was soon a proficient oarsman with bags of stamina.

By the summer of 1967, Fairfax was in peak physical condition, but still hadn't persuaded anyone to bankroll him. He placed an advertisement in *The Times* newspaper asking for help and waited for the donations to pour in. Of the six letters he received, only three were of any interest. A student offered to help with the boat-building, a family sent him a one pound banknote – Fairfax had it framed as a keepsake – and an amateur rower named Sylvia Cook offered her services as team secretary. Fairfax went to see Cook and within a few weeks they were dating and working together to organize his voyage.

It took another year for the couple to raise the money for the record-breaking attempt. Fairfax finally sailed from the Canary Islands on January 20, 1968, rowing *Britannia*, a 25 foot long, bright-orange boat made of mahogany coated with plastic. She was a self-righting, self-bailing, unsinkable tube weighed down with 100 days' worth of food, all carefully stored in watertight plastic wraps.

Fairfax landed on a Florida beach after a voyage lasting 180 days, swearing he'd never touch a pair of oars or eat another fish as long as he lived. The crossing had been much harder than he'd expected and he'd been forced to go hunting with his spear gun to supplement his rations. But, despite his pledge, on April 26, 1971, John Fairfax was rowing his heart out under the Golden Gate Bridge in San Francisco, bound for Australia. This time, Sylvia Cook had agreed to come along with him, to join in the adventure.

The contrasting personalities of Cook and Fairfax, trapped in the cramped space of *Britannia II*, would make wonderful material for a student psychologist. Fairfax was an indomitable, fearless and taciturn adventurer. He could sit in brooding silence for hours, puffing on his pipe, then suddenly he would jump up and dive over the side for a relaxing swim with a school of white tips. Cook was nervous about putting a toe in the water, overawed by the ocean and terrified of the toothy monsters she imagined stalking the boat. She was the planner and head chef, still putting in her fair share of hours at the oars. He was hunter and map-reader, one moment checking his speargun, the next taking a reading of the stars.

Fairfax was relying on celestial navigation to plot his way across the Pacific. He took great pride in his navigational skills and could plot his position on the globe to within five miles. His triumph in the Atlantic was all the more impressive because he'd chosen to cross at one of its widest points, and yet still managed to pilot his craft accurately, despite months of unpredictable currents and winds. The Pacific is almost four times wider than the Atlantic, but Fairfax was still confident of tracking their 12,000km (7,400 miles) route to Australia. He was so sure of his abilities, he told Cook he could direct the boat to one of the Pacific's myriad tiny atolls – little more than specks of dry land in the vastness of the ocean – in case of any emergency.

Celestial navigation is a complex business – one that involved Fairfax skipping around on the deck in his swimming trunks, stretching to get a clear view of the skies. He used a hand-held sextant, a device which measures the angle between the sun and the horizon. In overcast or squally weather it was impossible to take a reading. But if he could fix the angle then check the exact time on his Rolex wristwatch, a quick consultation of the tables in his pilot's books would give him his latitude. If he took a series of readings over a few hours, he could work out his longitude – by calculating the movement of the Sun over the given time.

It was a good thing Fairfax was an expert pilot. His land-finding skills would prove to be essential over the coming months.

The first weeks of the voyage were a shock to the system for Sylvia Cook. She had to adjust quickly to the mind-numbing boredom of four-hour shifts at the oars and get used to feeling constantly exhausted. The boat was cluttered and messy, swamped by huge waves and frequent downpours. None of this was good for her nerves, already strained tight as piano wire. The ocean is a noisy place. Every unexplained splash or sigh from the depths made her jump, while Fairfax didn't bat an eyelid if a huge whale broke the surface right next to them. There were few material comforts to soothe her. It was impossible to find anywhere comfortable to sit and she kept bumping into Fairfax every time she tried to move. To wash her long hair, Sylvia had to kneel over the side and dip her head into the waves, all the time convinced a shark was about to rear up out of the sea and lunge at her.

At the close of each day, the pair crawled into the hollow prow of *Britannia II*, a space they affectionately referred to as "the rathole". This cavity was less than three feet high and only six feet deep. It was usually soaking wet and always uncomfortable. But it was a place of refuge for Cook, somewhere to hide from the gales and pounding waves that had besieged their boat ever since they left the American coast. Even Fairfax was surprised at the violence of the weather. But he was more alarmed that his trusty Marconi radio wasn't transmitting properly. Unless they could send regular signals reporting their position, their sponsors – and families – would assume they were in danger. He decided to plot a course for land and on June 3, 1971, they anchored off a quiet Mexican bay, much to the amazement of the local fishermen.

For three weeks, Cook and Fairfax were minor celebrities around the port of Ensenada, making repairs to *Britoo* – their new nickname for their boat – and gathering fresh supplies. On June 27, they were at sea again, rowing into the great open jaws of the Pacific Ocean.

The Galley Slaves

By September, Sylvia Cook's doubts about life at sea had developed into an outright loathing for it. As *Britoo* meandered across the ocean at an average of 35 miles a day, she dreamed of her old life at home, her friends and family. The world she'd left behind seemed a paradise compared to this wasteland of blue water. Her body was showing all the scars of the typical ocean castaway: cracked lips, burned skin, cuts and bruises everywhere. The chaffing when she rowed was agony and, to make the friction burns worse, saltwater sores had broken out over her legs and arms. To top it all, her fear of the deep had never left her. She crawled around the pitching boat wearing a lifeline that was constantly getting tangled and cutting into her flesh. The only light entertainment on offer was adopting the fish that followed after the boat, freeloading dorados and pilot fish waiting for scraps. She made Fairfax promise not to spear any of her pets and gave them all names.

They had been rowing flat out for three months now and it was clear they needed a rest. On October 10, the 164th day of their voyage, they anchored off Washington Island (now Teraina) in the Western Pacific. Fairfax swam to shore over the island's reef and came back a few hours later with good news. The atoll was owned by an English company who farmed it for copra – crude coconut oil – and the plantation manager had invited them to stay with him as house guests. Even better, there were some cans of cold beer waiting for them on the beach.

For over a month they enjoyed a tranquil life on this palm-shaded Eden. Cook passed her time trying to learn some of the islanders' traditional crafts and studying their language. Fairfax went diving on the reef every morning, spearing hundreds of fish, a turtle and a manta ray twice his own weight.

The only drama came when *Britoo*'s anchor rope wrapped around some coral on the seabed. If the rope rubbed and shredded, the boat could drift onto the reef and break apart. Fairfax had to dive to a depth of 70 feet to free the anchor, and the crushing water pressure made his ears and nose stream with blood. The islanders who pulled him out of the surf afterwards were horrified by the sight of him. Fairfax casually explained that some of his blood vessels had ruptured, then strolled back to the house. After this escapade, he switched the anchor onto a steel cable.

They left the island on November 12, and Cook could not remember ever feeling more dejected. She felt an empathy with the tiny community encircled by the sea and had made some good friends among the islanders. For a moment she considered staying there, but deep down Cook was every bit as determined as Fairfax to finish their voyage to Australia. They resigned themselves to being galley slaves again, inching their way across the world's largest ocean.

On Christmas Day the sea was so wild they couldn't eat the luxury meal they'd saved for the occasion or set up the radio to call their relatives.

The Galley Slaves

They sat hunched in the rat hole, eating freeze-dried beef and beans, sipping on a coconut and a bottle of brandy. Their ordeal wore on into the New Year. But by early January, *Britoo's* freshwater supplies were dangerously low and Fairfax decided they should stop on one of the Gilbert Islands - now known as Kiribati - to restock. On January 9, 1972, they sighted the atoll Onotoa and Fairfax thought he saw a gap in its reef where they could enter. These island reefs are a terrible hazard for small boats, and sailors have to plot their approach routes precisely.

When they had rowed closer they saw a group of islanders on the beach waving to them. At first, they assumed this was just a friendly welcome but when Fairfax saw the line of white water raging ahead he realized it was a warning. The reef was much thicker than he'd first imagined and he couldn't see any safe channel leading to the beach.

They rowed with all their strength, trying to turn *Britoo* away from the breakers and the ledge of the razor-sharp reef ahead. But Onotoa's tidal currents were too strong and the boat lurched up to two massive coral heads, protruding from the breakers. *Britoo* was side-on to these prongs and about to be impaled. Peering into the spray, Fairfax saw a narrow gap in the reef. Without hesitating, he dived overboard, risking his life to turn his boat into the channel. He was almost pressed into the coral as *Britoo* swept over him but he had the satisfaction of seeing her float safely into the lagoon. She was still in one piece, but her hull was punctured and most of their equipment smashed and unusable.

Despite all their sufferings up to this point, it never crossed their minds to abandon the voyage. When they were told there was no equipment on Onotoa to carry out repairs, they arranged a tow to the larger island of Tarawa. By the time they left there on February 7, 1972, *Britoo* was seaworthy once more and their confidence had been restored after receiving the usual generous hospitality from the locals.

They were now into the last leg of their epic row. Surely, nothing could deny them victory now?

Sylvia Cook stared down at the wide gash the shark had made in Fairfax's arm. It was day 331 of their voyage and she thought she'd seen every hazard the ocean could throw at them. Since leaving Tarawa their radio had packed up, they'd survived dead calms, an electrical storm and heavy seas. Now Fairfax had been mauled by a shark. But she wasn't going to let it beat her. She was a more capable woman than she'd been at the beginning of all this.

Cook boiled some fresh water and waited for it to cool in the tropical heat. When it was tepid, she treated Fairfax to a slug of whisky and used the purified water to wash his wound. Next, she squirted a full tube of antiseptic cream over the bite and wrapped it tightly in a dressing and bandage. She'd made a good job of it, but was it going to be enough to prevent infection?

In the tropics, a tiny cut can become infected and suppurating in hours. Gangrene was a real threat and with no surgical equipment or proper drugs on board, Fairfax knew he would be lucky to survive an amputation. But the professional adventurer was tough. He concentrated all his willpower and great physical strength on beating the shark bite. When he noticed the barometer's level dropping rapidly and guessed a storm was coming, Fairfax didn't panic. Instead, he carefully lashed everything to the deck and told Cook to fetch the lifejackets.

"We'll ride it out, don't worry," he told her, ignoring the throbbing from his bandaged arm.

The storm raged for four days. Huddled together in the rathole, Cook and Fairfax watched waves cresting at over 26 feet high, on all sides of the boat. Each time *Britoo* dipped or rolled, Fairfax gulped in pain as his arm knocked against the hull. But he never gave up hope. Eventually, the storm must blow itself out and, with every day of high winds, *Britoo* was drifting closer to Australia.

On April 14, the cyclone had subsided and they found themselves lost inside a labyrinth of reefs. Fairfax quickly anchored in some shallow water and took a fix on the sun. They were barely 90 miles east of Australia. His arm was still aching but there was no sign of infection. If they could only pick their way through this maze of rocks and breaking waves, they could be on dry land in a matter of hours. For three days and nights they were cursed with indecision, worried that if they raised anchor they would crash onto the rocks and drown. Chance finally acted for them. Fairfax woke to find *Britoo* drifting. Her anchor cable had snapped – it was rusted and frayed after months of wear – and they were crashing through the reef on a rising tide. They could see the coral flying by, and at times the reef was only a few inches from *Britoo*'s keel. There was nothing to do but hang on to the rocking boat and pray she made it through to the open water.

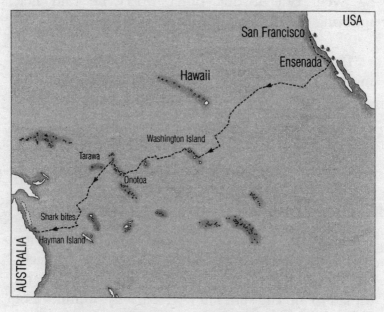

Map showing *Britoo*'s route across the Pacific

On April 22, 1972, after a voyage lasting 363 days, *Britoo* slid onto the sandy beach of Hayman Island, Australia. Cook and Fairfax stumbled ashore, into the grounds of a beach resort. They had broken several

The Galley Slaves

world records, rowing at least 13,000km (8,000 miles) and stopping only three times to make repairs or collect supplies. The galley slaves could lay down their oars at last.

Prisoners of the Sea

Waving to attract a passing ship

Maurice and Maralyn Bailey didn't look like a pair of globe-trotting sea adventurers. They were the kind of polite, well-dressed English couple you might expect to find tending their garden on a Sunday afternoon. Maurice was 41 and worked as a clerk with a printing company. Maralyn was 32, and had a job as a tax officer. Nothing in their appearance gave any hint that these two were longing to be sea dogs; Maralyn couldn't even swim. But looks can be deceptive. The Baileys had sea fever – and they were desperate to get out on the waves.

Since his teens, Maurice had loved the outdoor life and every weekend he'd go off camping, climbing or gliding. His need for adrenaline-raising adventure gradually infected Maralyn, and she craved a more thrilling existence than checking tax forms. But how could they escape the drudgery of their desk jobs? The promise of the oceans and a nomadic life under sail came rippling through their dreams as the solution.

There was only one problem with their yearning for the sea - money. Maurice paced around their house, explaining that it would be years before they'd be able to save enough to buy their own yacht.

"You're right," said Maralyn. "There's no getting around it."

"I'm afraid not," replied Maurice, nodding in resignation.

"Let's sell the house," Maralyn suggested breezily. "And we'll find new jobs on the coast and stay at a hotel until the boat's in a fit state to live in."

Maralyn had other plans as well - a voyage to New Zealand, and a new life when they got there. When Maurice got his breath back, he told her it was a brilliant idea. The Baileys were going to sea.

In June, 1972, they were ready to depart. Their 9m (31 foot) yacht, *Auralyn* - a blending of their Christian names - had been meticulously constructed and provisioned. Maralyn was particularly thorough and made sure that their floating home had every comfort. She was just as exacting with the safety equipment, insisting *Auralyn* carry an inflatable dinghy in addition to the regulation liferaft.

They sailed south, meandering towards Central America via ports in Spain, Portugal and the Canary Islands. *Auralyn* held up well in even the roughest weather and the Baileys soon adapted to life on the water. After nine months exploring the Atlantic they slipped through the Panama Canal and boldly set sail in the direction of the Galapagos Islands.

In the early morning of March 4, 1973, Maurice was coming down from his watch on deck when he noticed a pinpoint of light on the horizon.

"It must be a fisherman," he told Maralyn. "We're not far off land."

Their course took them closer to the light, until they could see it was indeed coming from a large fishing boat. Her crew was trailing a powerful searchlight beam across the waves.

"What are they up to?" asked Maralyn. But Maurice was equally puzzled.

"I think we'll press on," he told her. They sailed over the horizon, watching the mystery ship fade into the darkness.

At daybreak, Maurice woke to the familiar clatter of Maralyn preparing breakfast. He was just about to swing out of his bunk and join her when something smashed into the side of the cabin with the force of a speeding truck, slamming *Auralyn* across the waves. There was a cry from Maralyn, who had rushed to the deck.

"It's a whale, and I think he's injured."

Maurice darted up the cabin stairs and found himself standing in the shadow of a sperm whale's huge, dripping tail. Rolling in his own blood, the maddened animal could have crashed his body down onto *Auralyn*'s stern at any second. But, instead, he sounded below the waves, leaving behind only red, foaming water.

"I hope he's OK," whispered Maralyn.

"Never mind him," Maurice shouted. "We're taking water."

Sea water was lapping the bottom steps of the stairway. It took Maurice a few minutes to find the leak, wading around and feeling along the submerged planks with his fingers. The whale had kicked a hole in *Auralyn*'s port side, almost 18 inches square.

"We'll drag a sail over it," he shouted.

This emergency technique involves floating a spare sail across a leak and roping its corners to the cleats – fixing pegs – bolted into a yacht's deck. The canvas acts like a huge bandage. Under a perfect blue sky the Baileys hurried around their yacht, collecting a small sail and the necessary tools. When the sail was in position and drawn tight they worked the bilge pump for ten minutes, before checking the waterline in the cabin.

"It's still rising," cried Maralyn.

"The sail isn't holding," Maurice replied. "It's slipping off the hull."

"Let's stuff the leak with blankets," Maralyn ordered, still determined to save the yacht.

They waded across to the hull and worked frantically to plug the leak. It was no use. Even with the hole packed tight, the water kept rising. Only 40 minutes after the whale had rammed them, the Baileys accepted that *Auralyn* was going to sink.

They had ten minutes to collect their belongings: passports, food, water and survival equipment. Maralyn grabbed the emergency kit and methodically started selecting cans and packets from the galley and stuffing them into two sail bags. While she was busy below, Maurice dashed around the deck picking up as many water containers as he could carry. With *Auralyn* sinking under them, they roped the raft to the dingy and climbed in. Paying out a rope from the stern, the Baileys bobbed away from their cherished yacht. They took a series of photographs, last souvenirs of the ship they'd pinned all their hopes on, then sat in silence as she vanished into the depths.

"Those men this morning must have been whalers," said Maurice suddenly. "The blow to *Auralyn*'s hull didn't make the whale bleed. It was already wounded."

"That's what they were looking for," snapped Maralyn. "And the whale attacked us because it thought we were the hunters."

They were silent again, too stunned by the loss of the yacht to consider their predicament. It was Maralyn who first asked the question: "How soon will we be rescued?"

Maurice made a quick appraisal of their situation. They were roughly 480km (300 miles) northeast of the Galapagos Islands and not far from a busy shipping lane. There was enough food and water to last them about 20 days, some flares, a flashlight – even a sextant and his wristwatch to help chart their position. But he still wasn't optimistic about their chances. Maurice knew that the prevailing currents and winds would carry them to the northwest, out into the vast emptiness of the Pacific. He was also aware that they were only a tiny shape on the sea, too small to be picked up by surface radar and difficult for any passing sailor to notice. He couldn't bring himself to tell this to Maralyn, so he racked his mind for an idea that might help them.

"What about rowing to the islands?" he said suddenly.

"All the way to the Galapagos?" Maralyn cried.

"Why not? We're drifting towards the northwest," he explained. "In about ten days we'll be north of the Galapagos and we'll have missed them. But if we row one hundred miles due south, to counteract the drift, we should wash up there."

"Let's get started then," said Maralyn confidently. Even suffering a shipwreck hadn't dented her optimism.

"Tomorrow might be better," Maurice suggested. "We'll have drifted onto the shipping lane by then and, if we're rescued, we'll have tired ourselves out for nothing. Let's try to get some rest."

The raft was too small for them both to lie down at the same time. So, they took turns sleeping, taking three-hour watches as they had on *Auralyn*. It was their first night in the liferaft and it was just as uncomfortable as they'd feared.

They woke to feel the searing equatorial sun baking the walls of their little orange capsule. There were no ships in sight when they drew back the raft's rubberized canopy, nothing but sky and open water. To console themselves, they drew up their daily menu: biscuits spread with margarine and marmalade for breakfast, a few peanuts for lunch and a can from the galley for dinner. Maralyn had brought a small gas burner from the yacht to heat the cans. A hot meal was a luxury they shared by moonlight, taking turns dipping a spoon into such delights as curry or steak and kidney pudding. They had around a dozen cans of food and almost enough gas to heat them all. Surely this would do until they were rescued?

Maurice had salvaged ten gallons of drinking water from the yacht, but on inspection he discovered that the sea had ruined four of them. They allowed themselves a pint a day, sipping at it through the afternoon.

The air temperature cooled when night came and they began rowing. It was exhausting work, propelling the raft and dinghy across the waves. To make matters worse, the exertion made them thirsty. Maralyn doubled the water ration. After eight hours of taking turns at the oars they fell into the raft and tried to sleep.

In the morning, Maurice calculated their progress with the sextant. All their sweating at the oars had carried them only 6km (4 miles) south. Maurice couldn't bring himself to crush Maralyn's hopes, so he said nothing. Perhaps they would do better in the days to come?

But after another two nights of hard work, they had only managed to push 16km (10 miles) to the south. Maurice confessed to Maralyn that there was no point in rowing that evening – they were sweeping past the northern tip of the islands and powerless to prevent it.

"We'll still be in the shipping lane, though," said Maralyn cheerfully. "A boat will pick us up in no time at all."

"That's right," he answered, with a forced smile.

The week passed slowly, with few distractions from the tropical heat and the long hours between meals. One surprise was a visit from a small turtle, nibbling at the underside of the raft.

"They must be attracted to the shade," laughed Maurice.

"Let's catch it," replied Maralyn.

A moment later the animal was trapped inside the rubber walls of the dinghy.

"We could eat it," said Maralyn, "or use it as bait to catch fish."

"We haven't got any fish hooks," sighed Maurice.

"No, but I've got some safety pins somewhere," she answered, rummaging through the sacks. "We could bend them into hooks and there's an eye at the end to take some thread."

"Let's wait until the cans run out before we think about anything as gruesome as that," replied Maurice.

At breakfast on their eighth day as castaways, Maralyn saw a ship.

"Get the flares," she shouted, "we're saved."

Maurice pulled the dinghy closer so they would make a bigger target for searching eyes, then tugged on a flare. But nothing happened and he threw it into the sea in disgust.

"Try another," cried Maralyn, who was waving her oilskin jacket overhead and shouting at the top of her lungs. The second flare burst into life and Maurice waved it in an arc.

"They must see that," shouted Maralyn. But the ship kept thundering through the waves on its course, less than two miles away. "Light another one."

Maurice lit three more flares, but the ship was blind to them all. It dropped over the horizon and they were alone again with the sea.

"Perhaps the crew was all down below having breakfast," said Maralyn.

"Or perhaps they just weren't looking," replied Maurice gloomily.

One of the most depressing things for people in a survival craft is to realize how invisible they are on the ocean. In the ever-changing seascape of shadows, waves and spray, a small raft is surprisingly hard to spot. Shipwrecked sailors spend hours studying the limits of their watery world. For them, there is nothing more vital than keeping a close watch out for a rescue ship. Their lives depend on it. But, for the hard-working crew of a trawler or cargo boat, the ocean is a blank canvas. They could be at sea for months without sighting another vessel. Although maritime law has strict guidelines about keeping

119

watch at sea, many ships just set the autopilot and hope for the best.

The Baileys had two flares left, half the food stocks salvaged from the yacht were gone and their water supply was fast running out. Maurice knew that if it didn't rain soon they would have to cut the daily ration. That evening, to rub salt in the wounds of a miserable day, their gas ran out and they had to eat from a cold can.

They both knew it was time to try fishing. For that they needed bait and their attention turned to the captive turtle.

It was a clumsy assassination. They started at first light, whacking the poor reptile over the head with a paddle. It fell stunned and Maurice grabbed it by the rear flippers, holding its head over a bowl. Now Maralyn joined the fray, hacking at the beast's throat with a blunt knife – this and some scissors were their only cutting tools. To her horror, the turtle skin was as hard as leather and wouldn't yield to her blade. As she sawed away at its neck, their victim came around and started thrashing about in a flipper-frenzy until Maralyn finally sank the knife deep into its throat, drenching herself in blood.

They turned the body over and started cutting around the perimeter of the shell. This took even longer than the execution, but when it was done they removed four large steaks of white meat. Sickened by the gore, Maralyn dumped the carcass over the side, attracting a swarm of carnivorous fish.

It was time to cast a line. After baiting a safety pin with chunks of turtle meat, they caught several trigger fish in less than a minute. While Maralyn took care of the angling, Maurice was chef. Soon, they'd collected a neat pile of white fillets and were ready to try a dinner of *sashimi* – raw fish.

Maralyn could only stomach a bite or two, but Maurice dived in. He found the eyeballs particularly delicious – and very thirst-quenching.

Reassured that they wouldn't starve as long as they could keep hooking fish, the Baileys set about solving another problem that often plagues castaways – boredom. Aside from spending hours playing word games or torturing one another with descriptions of lavish restaurant meals, there was little to occupy their minds. Maralyn took on the role of entertainment officer with her usual enthusiasm. She made a domino set from the pages of her notebook, and when this was a success she fabricated a complete pack of playing cards. The Baileys played endless card games as they drifted around the Pacific. Maralyn also remembered a story she'd read about an American pilot who had been kept in solitary confinement when his plane crashed in enemy territory. To keep himself sane, he set about building a dream house in his imagination, down to the position of every last nail. Maralyn raised the possibility of designing their new yacht, but she was unsure of Maurice's reaction. To her delight, he was just as keen on the plan. The Baileys had lost

Auralyn, but they hadn't lost their love for the sea. They started drawing diagrams of *Auralyn II*, and their conversations about her design were another welcome activity.

On March 21, after 17 days in the raft, they had their first rainstorm. Maurice placed a bucket under a steady drip from the canopy and they collected about a pint. Eagerly they swallowed great gulps of the liquid – and then spat it out. The rubber coating on the raft made it taste disgusting. Undaunted, they tried again. The next pint was much better, although the water they collected always retained this rubbery aftertaste. In the evening they caught another turtle and quickly dissected it. This time they were more adventurous and ate much more of the creature, including its green body fat. Hunger was making them less squeamish about their diet.

Maralyn saw the second ship on March 29. It was the middle of the night and Maralyn thought this would make their flares stand out, ensuring their rescue. The first flare was another dud, but the second lit up the sea all around them. By now the ship was so close they could see its portholes and the bright compartments beckoning from within.

The ship sailed on.

"Third time lucky," whispered Maralyn, clinging on to hope despite her disappointment.

By the end of May, the Baileys had seen seven ships and they still hadn't been rescued. After 90 days in the raft their bodies were emaciated and covered in saltwater sores. Neither of them were good swimmers, and because they were forced to crouch most of the time the muscles in their legs had wasted away. Their clothes were little better than rags. Even the raft was starting to decay. Its glued seams had split and the canopy was no longer waterproof. It was a constant battle to keep anything dry.

When they passed the hundred day mark, the Baileys had regressed to a form of "primeval" existence. All their energies were concentrated on catching food and protecting the tiny rubber craft that supported them over the blue abyss below. Maralyn adapted herself to every problem and never lost her will to live. She was convinced that their ordeal had some purpose or meaning and forced herself to survive. She caught birds that landed on the raft to preen themselves and became an expert angler, even capturing small sharks. Maurice didn't have his wife's sustaining willpower, but his respect for her optimism and lust for life kept him going. He couldn't bear the thought of leaving Maralyn alone in the raft, so he put up with the hardship.

They drifted through storms and dead calms, slowly forging a close relationship with the sea. The ocean was their world – it fed them, slaked their thirsts and used up every last grain of their strength. It also thrilled them. The Baileys were treated to a startling display of marine life: fields of plankton in a glass-still sea, rare basking sharks, whales, dolphins and schools of tropical fish.

They never stopped making plans for the future. Maralyn had asked Maurice where he would like to go when *Auralyn II* was ready for her maiden voyage. The question had grown into another ambitious plan – to visit Patagonia and chart some of Chile's wild southern coast. The Baileys willed themselves to go on living, so they could turn these shared dreams into a reality.

In the afternoon of June 30, Maralyn sighted a small, white ship approaching them. She started waving her jacket, encouraging an exhausted Maurice to do the same. The ship came closer, until it passed only half a mile from the raft. It kept going.

"It's no good," cried Maurice, dropping his jacket. "They're not stopping. Save your strength."

"No, just a bit longer," she shouted. "They must see us."

Maurice could only stare up at his wife with pride, while she continued waving desperately.

"They're turning," she whispered. "They're coming back for us."

He lifted his head over the side of the raft. The ship had stopped on the waves. Its bow was slowly coming around.

"They've seen us," she cried.

A few minutes later they were being helped aboard a Korean trawler, strong arms pulling them onto the deck. The Baileys were too weak to stand. They collapsed onto some mats and one of the sailors brought glasses of hot milk. Maralyn still had enough strength left to thank their rescuers.

They had survived 117 days adrift in a liferaft not much bigger than a bathtub – and this was only the beginning of their adventures. The Baileys went on to build *Auralyn II* and explore the coast of Patagonia and other wild shores – just as they had promised themselves when they were prisoners of the sea.

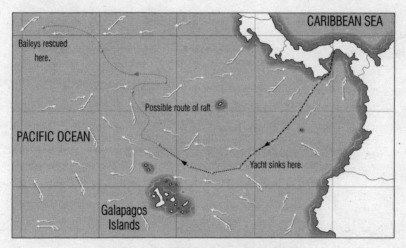

Map showing the Baileys drifting in the Pacific
The arrows show ocean currents.

Swimming with the Fishes

Captain Webb saw the sailor lose his grip in the high rigging and smash down into the rolling mid-Atlantic waves. There was a gale coming and the sea was already wild. Even if the man wasn't torn apart by the ship's huge propellers he'd have to be a strong swimmer to survive on the ocean swell. Without a second thought for his own safety, Webb pulled his seaman's jacket off, put a foot on the wooden handrail and dived over the side. It was 1873 and the ship, the *Russia*, was one of the fastest passenger liners in service, crossing from New York to Cork in southern Ireland in just eight days. As Webb surfaced he saw her slice past and steam away. He could only hope that a passenger or crewman had witnessed the accident and was rushing to alert the ship's captain.

Webb started swimming to where he'd seen the sailor enter the water. He thought he could see a head, cresting on the white-tipped waves. But when he reached the spot all he found was a torn sailor's cap. The man had already sunk below, leaving Captain Webb bobbing alone on the surface.

For 37 minutes, he swam in circles, craning his neck over the rollers in search of the ship. He wasn't in the least bit scared or intimidated by the mighty ocean. To his surprise, the experience seemed no different from his other swimming exploits. For years, Webb had prided himself on his incredible stamina in the open water. One summer, at Southsea Beach on England's south coast, he'd argued with a man about the strength of dogs as swimmers. His opponent was confident that his Newfoundland hound could beat any man in an endurance contest. Webb challenged him and his canine companion to a bet – and won. After an hour and a half treading water in a heavy sea, the dog paddled over to his owner's boat and whimpered until he was lifted in.

For these 37 minutes in the Atlantic, Webb was alone with his thoughts. The cold bothered him slightly, but aside from that he was perfectly comfortable. "I could swim for hours in this," he said to himself. An idea suddenly flashed into his mind, something he'd been wondering about trying for years, a feat the experts said was humanly impossible.

When one of the *Russia's* longboats finally arrived to haul him out, Webb had made a decision that would change his life forever. His time in the freezing ocean was all the encouragement he'd needed. Captain Webb was going to swim the English Channel.

The Channel – *Oceanus Britannicus* – has played a part in almost every noteworthy event in Britain's war-torn history. Around 560km (350 miles) long, but only 34km (21 miles) wide at its narrowest point, it has been a frustrating obstacle to every impatient invader. Napoleon stood on the beach at Cape Gris-Nez, berating his admirals: "If I can see the coast of England, why is it so difficult for you to get my army over there?"

His trembling subordinates could hardly explain that the puzzling character of the Channel – and perhaps that of the British people – comes down to a single issue: the weather. Although the Channel is narrow, it is relatively shallow for a stretch of sea – most of its floor is no deeper than 122m (400 feet). This, combined with a peculiar tidal system, and the unpredictable British climate, make it a nightmare for shipping. Its waters can change from a glassy pool to a raging storm in minutes.

Napoleon was not the only tyrant to be thwarted by it. Hitler's Panzer divisions and King Philip II's Spanish Armada couldn't make it across either. Shrouded in fog, crisscrossed by dangerous currents and rushing tides, the Channel is a formidable body of water, even for a stout ship. In the 1870s, anyone thinking of swimming between England and France was mocked as a fool or a madman. To have any chance of success, he or she would need some very special talents.

Matthew Webb was born in January 1848, in a small town close to the Severn River – Britain's longest waterway. As soon as he could walk, he was playing in the river shallows and by the time he was nine years old he'd staged his first rescue, saving his younger brother from drowning. Webb had no flair or great speed in the water; he was a plodder, sticking to a slow, rhythmic breaststroke. Barrel-chested and chubby, the other boys laughed at him when he challenged them to long-distance races. But Webb was indefatigable and he never lost. Indeed, he soon became a bit of a show-off.

His love for the water influenced his choice of career and, when he was 12, Webb signed up for the merchant navy. During a dozen years of service around the world, he never missed a chance to display his remarkable powers. When his ship's anchor was fouled by a rope in the Suez Canal, he spent two hours diving underwater to cut it free. He saved a naval cadet from drowning and received danger money from a South African salvage company for swimming through rough seas that every other sailor on his ship had refused to enter. After his rescue attempt from the *Russia*, Webb was awarded a gold medal for bravery by the Duke of Edinburgh and prize money made up from public donations. The Captain was growing to like the sound of applause and the rustle of banknotes. In the summer of 1874, he started preparations for the swim he hoped would make his name and fortune – Dover to Calais across the Channel.

He began with a secret study of the terrain, like a spy taking notes on an enemy fortification. Webb moved to the coastal town of Folkstone and was up early with the morning crowds, walking briskly to his work. The sea glinted below him, a block of blue glimpsed between shopfronts, cheap boarding houses and public bars. But, instead of a briefcase or sack of tools under his arm, Captain Webb carried a bag of beef sandwiches wrapped in a small towel. This was all he needed for his day's work. When he reached the beach he walked along the sand until he found a deserted spot. Webb didn't want to be disturbed. He slipped out of his clothes, leaving a neat pile on the towel, then stepped into the waves.

Over the next weeks he tested his staying power in the chilly waters of the Channel. For most people, a few hours floating in these low temperatures – around 12°C (53°F) – brought stiffness in their joints, headaches, drowsiness and then mental confusion as they developed hypothermia. But Webb had an iron constitution. When he'd tried a few 9km (6 mile) swims without succumbing to cramps, nausea or tiredness, he was sure he could make the 34km (21 miles) to the French coast. He hurried back to London to drum up support for his plan, but the reaction was lukewarm at best. London swimming groups still didn't think the crossing was possible.

This wasn't the only disappointment for Webb. Other people had eyes on a Channel victory as well – he had competition from America.

There had already been one attempt on the Channel before Webb decided to throw his hat into the ring. In 1872, the captain of Hyde Park's Serpentine Swimming Club lasted an hour in the water before clambering into a motor launch, blue with cold. The new challenger, Pennsylvanian Paul Boyton, wasn't foolish enough to believe the Channel could be conquered unaided. He would be wearing an inflatable rubber suit, designed to save shipwrecked passengers. This bizarre invention looked a little like a modern diving suit, with only the swimmer's face and hands uncovered. It had air chambers arranged under the rubber, a hook mounted near the ankle that held a mini-sail, and it came supplied with a paddle, so the castaway could row themselves to dry land.

It might have looked odd, but the suit was effective. In May 1875, Boyton paddled onto Dover beach after crossing from France. He didn't quite steal the Channel swimming crown. After all, he had had the benefit of the rubber suit and an oar. But the flamboyant American - he liked to lie back and smoke a cigar during breaks from his paddling duties - certainly roused the public's interest. Boyton's success made Webb even more determined to be the first man to swim unaided across Britain's most famous stretch of water, and in August 1875 he was ready to make the attempt.

From the beginning, it was an ill-timed and unlucky venture. Webb had assembled a coterie of journalists and artists - the photographers of their times - in the lounge of his Dover hotel. They pressured him to begin the swim, even though the local Channel pilot that Webb had hired warned against it because of threatening clouds. For weeks the sea had been choppy and menaced by sudden squalls. Webb cancelled two start dates, but on the third morning – August 12 – he refused to delay any longer. Rubbing himself all over with greasy porpoise oil – as foul-smelling as it sounds – Webb set off from Dover's Admiralty Pier, accompanied by a yacht with a crew of six and a pack of pressmen aboard. He also had two friends in a small boat who would row across the Channel and remain by his side.

After four hours in the water, he'd made 11km (7 miles) and was still going strong. But the sea was crashing around him and the men in the boats were terribly seasick. Suddenly, a squall blew up, bringing a deluge of rain that was so thick Webb could barely see his hands in front of his face. The captain of the yacht realized that a storm was setting in and advised Webb to give up the attempt. Although he had all his strength left, Webb conceded that he was being "blown about like a shuttlecock" and was worried for the safety of the men in the smaller boat. He pulled himself into the yacht, accepting that the elements had beaten him.

Webb returned to Dover a loser, but he didn't pack his bags and leave. The race was still on. He waited for the weather to change, checking the clouds and the ocean horizon every morning. On August 24, after a long consultation with his crew, he decided that, as last, the conditions were right for another attempt.

Sporting only a pair of scarlet trunks, and smothered in more porpoise oil, Webb dived off the

Admiralty Pier at five minutes past noon. He was escorted once again by the two boats, their crews and a few members of the press. In contrast with the stormy weather of his last attempt, there wasn't a ripple on the sea. In fact, it was so warm a haze of low cloud obscured the French coast. Webb settled into a slow rhythm of 20 strokes per minute, conscious that he had to pace himself for the marathon swim ahead.

After four hours, he had managed 8km (5 miles), but the Channel's tides were turning and Webb soon found the going a lot harder. He stopped for some beef tea, fortified with strong ale. Most long-distance swimmers in Webb's times were fond of an alcoholic tipple out on the waves. Brandy, whisky and beer were all popular. Webb had even had a glass of red wine with his breakfast of ham and eggs that morning.

The Channel was a crowded shipping lane – today it's the world's busiest – and at six in the evening a French steamer, *Ville de Maga*, churned past while the sailors on board stared goggle-eyed at the tubby swimmer. Webb's team was furious that "the foreigners" hadn't cheered their man on. They soothed themselves by digging into some fried eggs and cracking open a keg of beer.

Webb requested a drink of hot coffee at half past eight. The sea was dark now, except for the flicker of the yacht's gas lanterns across the waves, but this didn't unsettle him. His only complaint at this stage was that he was covered in trailing seaweed and it weighed him down. But around nine o'clock he was yelping in pain – a jellyfish had stung him on the shoulder. Schools of these jellyfish cluster in the middle of the Channel and Webb might have congratulated himself on getting this far. But he was probably too distracted by the pain to realize he'd reached the halfway mark. There was no doctor with his team – Webb was so confident he had thought it unnecessary to invite one – but the crew passed him some brandy which he rubbed all over the sting. He swam on and was stung again an hour later. But, although the number of his strokes per minute dropped slightly, he seemed as strong as ever.

Just before midnight Webb received a welcome boost to his morale when the steamer *Maid of Kent* came up alongside the yacht. She had broken her journey to Calais so her passengers could show their support; 300 of them gathered on the decks to cheer Webb along. He was only 11km (7 miles) from the French coast and the tide was still against him. When it finally turned – around 3:00am – it was a mixed blessing, as it brought a high wind, stirring up the sea. By 5:00am he was flagging, and signalled for more beef tea and some brandy. Webb's voice sounded weak and his team wondered if he could last much longer in the choppy waves. To help him, they positioned the boats against the wind and Webb swam on the protected leeward side. The Captain pushed on, relying on his reserves of "bulldog pluck" to keep going. At 8:00am he drank some more brandy and raised his stroke speed to 22 per minute, with the town of Calais looming tantalizingly close. But the last mile was the hardest. Webb's arms and shoulders were aching and sore, his eyes blurry and stinging with all the sea spray, and each wave seemed to throw him back, away from the beach. Perhaps guessing he was in difficulty, the captain of the *Maid of Kent* came out from the port in another boat and stayed on Webb's weather side, calming the waters with her bulk.

Towards 10:00am Webb's stroke count had gone up to 26 per minute, but his movements were weak and flailing compared to his earlier style. The sound of cheers from the shore lifted his spirits and at 10:30am he was cracking jokes with his crew.

"Let's hope the Frenchmen have got some decent grub waiting for me," he called.

Finally, at 10:40am Greenwich Mean Time, Captain Webb felt the sand oozing between his toes and stumbled onto the bathing beach at Calais. He had been in the water for almost 22 hours and covered a total distance of 63km (39 miles) as he weaved across the Channel. A great crowd was waiting for him on the beach, but Webb was in no fit state for speeches or celebrations. He climbed into a horse-drawn carriage and was driven straight to the Hotel de Paris, where he fell into a deep sleep that lasted 15 hours.

When he checked out the next day, the landlord had the nerve to demand 50 francs for "medical attention" - which had consisted of nothing more than a doctor measuring his pulse.

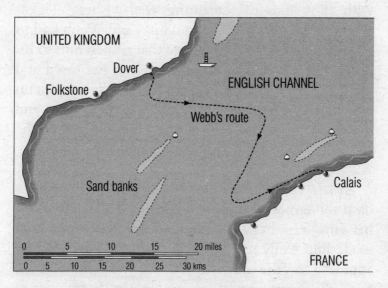

UNITED KINGDOM

Dover

Folkstone

ENGLISH CHANNEL

Webb's route

Sand banks

Calais

0   5   10   15   20 miles
0   5   10   15   20   25   30 kms

FRANCE

Map showing Captain Webb's Channel crossing swim

"I'm afraid I arrived in Calais with only my swimming trunks," replied Webb. "But the next time I swim over I'll pay you."

Webb had survived his Channel adventure with no greater injuries than jellyfish stings and some chaffing around his neck and arms. He returned to Dover thrilled by his success, but still feeling essentially unchanged by the experience. But he was wrong. He would never escape the fact that he was a man defined by one spectacular achievement – the man who had swum the Channel.

It all began sensationally. Webb was a star. The drab pier that had been his starting point was covered with thousands of screaming well-wishers. Ticker tape and flags decked the buildings and Webb had to escape the crowds in a carriage that rushed him to his hotel. For a week he was the toast of the town and his name was splashed across the headlines. Britain was immensely proud of Webb's achievement and the Press presented him as the embodiment of the Victorian ideals of a strong body and strong mind.

At last, tiring of the Dover carnival, Webb made a dash for London. But he was harried all the way by his fans. His huge moustache and burly physique made him easily recognizable from the portraits that appeared in the newspapers. He was mobbed on train platforms, street corners, in the back seats of taxis – even in the London Stock Exchange, which he had visited to invest the money that came flooding in from an adoring public. For the best part of six months, Webb was a celebrity around London and his life was a whirl of regimental dinners, award ceremonies and interviews. But, by the spring of 1876, his star had waned, and the captain was left wondering: "What next?"

In an effort to prolong his fame, Webb tried writing books on swimming technique and hiring lecture halls to give talks about his epic swim. But he was fast becoming yesterday's news. The crowds stayed away. This bruised his ego and his purse. Webb needed money. Although he'd been given more than £2000 – worth more than a hundred times that today – it was all invested, and the annual income it provided wasn't enough to fund his lifestyle. The Channel title was at least safe: no swimmer would make it across for another 36 years. But Webb frittered his time away with no clear direction to his career.

To make some quick cash he took part in endurance competitions, tawdry sideshows that had him bobbing around in aquarium tanks for six days at a time while spectators paid a penny to gawp. There were other, equally silly, competitions and demonstrations of his stamina. He began appearing in races along the east coast of America, sponsored by tavern owners or hoteliers. By 1883 his health was deteriorating, ravaged by too many senseless swims that had earned him very little. For years he had known that the only way to restore his fame was to undertake another great challenge, something to surpass his Channel achievement. Like a punch-drunk boxer determined to go into the ring for one last, disastrous fight, Webb announced that he would swim across the Niagara Falls whirlpool.

The Niagara Falls is the third largest natural waterfall in the world, a wide rim of cascading water along the border between the United States and Canada. At the base of the falls, the Niagara river sluices down into a huge whirlpool in a roaring crush of white water. Webb coolly announced that he would swim through the river's rapids, cross the whirlpool and land on the shore beyond.

His friends begged him to be sensible. It would be suicide to go into the water. If he survived the rapids – which could snap great logs in two – the whirlpool would rip him to pieces. But Webb had always been his own man, and he was determined to go ahead with the challenge. He needed money and claimed that the event would earn him $10,000 or more. When a local reporter challenged him on this point, Webb confessed that he had been exaggerating. He had tried to coax some cash out of the railway companies and local merchants, telling them they would benefit by an increase of customers watching his challenge, but they'd turned him down flat. Webb was really only doing it to show that he was the world's best swimmer. To back down now would tarnish his reputation forever.

On July 24, 1883, Captain Webb swam boldly into the rapids and vanished from sight. His body was discovered four days later, washed up in a quiet cove. The water had finally beaten him, but it could never eclipse the heroism he'd shown swimming the English Channel.

Fountain of Gold

"Johnno" Johnstone had his nose pressed against one of the quartz observation windows when he heard a sickening clunk echo through the water around him. He'd been diving professionally for so many years he didn't need to guess what had happened. His ship, the *Claymore*, had lost the anchor that kept her fixed in position over the wreck he was inspecting. Without the anchor, the *Claymore* would drift on the Pacific waves. Johnstone was in a diving bell, 134m (438 feet) down, hanging like a puppet on a string from one of the ship's cranes.

He felt a sudden lurch, then he saw the steel plates of the wreck's hull rushing towards him. At the last second, the bell lifted and cleared the side of the wreck, almost brushing the twisted steel snags of the deck railings. If the bell or any of her windows were holed, Johnstone would drown in seconds. Should the line to the crane snare or catch on anything, he would be trapped on the wreck until his air ran out. With his heart in his mouth, Johnstone watched as the bell cleared the deck and tumbled over the far side. Before he could breathe a sigh of relief, he found himself dropping towards a great, black hole in the wreck's keel. It was a blast from a German mine that had sent the ship to the bottom. Johnstone stared into the depths of a bomb crater, so close he could see the torn steel plating of the ship's inner decks. For a second the bell hung there, almost resting on the rim of the hole. Finally it pulled away, slammed into the seabed and was still.

Up on the surface, Captain John Williams realized the *Claymore* was drifting.

"Up the bell, full speed," he shouted to his men.

He watched the steel line go taught and begin to coil around the drum. It took seven minutes to lift the diving chamber. When it finally arrived, every man in the crew was silent while a mechanic scrambled on top of the dripping tube and kicked at the release bolts. The lid of the bell swung open and Johnstone stuck his head out. He had a few cuts on his face and was badly shaken, but he still had the strength to climb out unaided and jump down onto the deck.

"Don't let that happen again," he roared at the assembled sailors, "don't *ever* let that happen again."

In the early morning of June 19, 1940, the trans-Pacific liner *Niagara* had steamed straight into a German sea mine. She was only four hours out of Auckland, New Zealand, and nobody had expected an enemy raider to lay mines more than 19,000km (12,000 miles) from the battle zones of Europe. But the *Niagara* sank, and although all her passengers and crew were saved, her loss was a disaster for the British government. As part of her cargo, the ship had been secretly transporting 590 solid gold bars to America, to help pay for essential munitions and supplies. This treasure was packed in small wooden crates and was worth millions, even then. The British were determined to recover it. They asked around for a salvage man who might be up to the task and one name kept coming up: Captain John Williams.

Williams was a grizzled veteran of the great age of sail. He'd seen the renowned *Cutty Sark* when he was a boy and its grace and grandeur had inspired him to go to sea. Working his way up from crewman to captain, Williams had been sunk twice by German U-boats during the First World War and explored every corner of the globe before setting up his company, United Salvage, in Melbourne, Australia. He made a careful study of the *Niagara*'s design and likely position and announced boldly:

"It's a tough nut, but I think I can crack it."

Williams was under no illusions about the difficulty of his mission. The *Niagara* had sunk in an area well known for sudden storms, about 45km (28 miles) off the northeast coast of New Zealand. She was lying in water up to 134m (440 feet) deep – yet in 1940 the deepest salvage operation involving diving equipment had only ever managed to reach as far as 122m (400 feet). And it had been a complex undertaking. Because of the crushing water pressure at these depths, the diver had to be lowered inside a protective metal bell. He took with him a supply of oxygen and a crude telephone system connected to the dive ship. The ship itself was anchored to six concrete blocks, each placed accurately on the seabed to form a perimeter around the wreck. Mooring the dive ship was a little like putting a dart in a bull's-eye – and not much easier. But, despite the extra depth, Williams thought he could use the same techniques to salvage the *Niagara*.

He outlined his plan to his Bank of England sponsors. With the diver acting as an observer, his team would begin blasting into the side of the wreck, trying to dig down to the strongroom where the gold was stored. Each explosive charge would have to be carefully positioned by means of a line and crane, mounted on the ship's swaying deck. When the strongroom was eventually exposed, the team would use a steel-toothed grab to scoop out its treasure. If they were lucky, they would find the gold bullion where it had been stored, but Williams offered no guarantees. All too often the violence of a sinking dislodges a ship's cargo, sending it crashing to another part of the craft.

As if all this wasn't nerve-wracking enough, there was a war going on. The sea around the *Niagara* was still full of mines – and perhaps enemy submarines – and every able ship and sailor in the region was required for other duties. Williams knew that the first thing he'd need was a suitable diving ship. He set off for New Zealand, trying to be optimistic about what he'd find.

It was worse than he'd imagined. After visiting three crumbling hulks that were barely able to float, Williams was ready to give up and go home. His shipping agent asked him to see one more boat before he packed his bags – a "bit of a character" that had been decommissioned at the start of the war.

The *Claymore* was a dirty tub of a steamer, lying abandoned in the mud off Auckland docks. She was 40 years old and every inch of her showed it. In her prime, she had carried passengers and freight, and was praised for her speed and luxury. Her saloon rooms were lined with walnut panelling and red velvet trim. There was even some stained glass displaying McGregor tartan. But those were the glory days. Now the *Claymore*'s superstructure was rotting away with neglect. Grass sprouted through her sagging decks and hordes of rats skittered along her passageways. Williams watched gulls landing in the funnel, tending to their nests.

"How are her engines?" he asked the shipping agent.

"In good order. But the boiler's weak and there's a blade missing from the propellor. She'll only do five knots."

Williams kicked the old ship's metal hull with his boot. It rang solid.

"She'll do just fine."

Williams was canny and wise; he knew that under all her grime and decay the *Claymore* was still a strong ship. He began fitting her out for the mission, scrounging equipment wherever he could find it. Everything was begged or borrowed, with one exception – the diving bell had to be custom-made. It was tubular, cast from manganese bronze and steel

145

and stood 3m (9 feet) high. There were 14 quartz observation windows set around its neck and an array of dials and controls mounted on the inside walls. Williams realized the success of the mission depended on the quality of his divers, and he was lucky to recruit the best – "Johnno" Johnstone and his brother Bill.

"Johnno" was something of a living legend among salvage experts. He was born in the English port of Liverpool, and learned his underwater skills while training with an elite navy diving squad during the First World War. After the war, he'd been drawn to Australia in search of adventure. Tall, lanky and always relaxed, he was known as a patient and meticulous diver with nerves of steel.

One Johnno anecdote described how he was stalked by a groper – a huge, deep-water fish, related to the cod family – while diving off a wreck in the South Seas. Gropers hide in caves or under rocks and are just as quick and aggressive as barracudas. When Johnno realized he was being tracked around the wreck by the fish, he went to the surface and collected a stick of explosive from the dive ship. Returning to the bottom, he turned hunter, following the groper until it settled in the mouth of a cave. At any second the fish could have attacked, but Johnstone calmly set the charge among some nearby rocks and made for his ship. After he'd triggered the explosion, the groper floated up to the waves. But it was only stunned. Johnstone had to chase after his prey, stab it several times and finally drag it to the deck on the end of a steel cable. The fish was 2m (7 feet) long and weighed 226kg (500lbs). Johnstone mounted it as a trophy in his house in Melbourne, where it struck terror into his guests.

Williams' first challenge was to find the wreck. With a motley crew of youths and old sea salts manning the *Claymore*, he began scouring the ocean on December 19, 1940. The ship started working her way around a 6km (4 miles) sided square, towing a steel scraper along the sea floor. From the *Niagara*'s log and her passengers' statements, Williams had calculated the ship had sunk somewhere within this cube of water. He prowled around his bridge, waiting for the scraper to catch on the wreck.

On December 29, the *Claymore* had her first bite. The scraper held fast against some object and Williams immediately dropped anchor and sent Johnno down to take a look.

"What can you see?" the captain whispered into his mouthpiece.

"Not much," replied Johnno, his voice a crackle coming up from the deep. "The light's not too good down here. There might be a rock. Yes, that must have been it."

"Up the bell," Williams shouted to the deck hands, eager to resume the search. "And raise anchor."

"Captain," one of the sailors shouted. "There's something coming up with the anchor cable."

Williams rushed down from the bridge to take a look. Perhaps they'd found the wreck after all?

"Stop the winch," he growled. "Can't you see what it is?"

"I don't know sir," replied the sailor. "It looks like a clump of weeds hanging under the surface."

Williams' blood ran cold as he stared at the murky shape below the waves. "Weeds, you say?" he cried. "That's a mine."

Every man on the *Claymore* clustered around their captain to take a look. They could see the mine's detonator "horns" several feet down, poking through a mass of seaweed.

"We'll have to cut it loose," cried one man. "It's wrapped around the anchor."

"That's no good," answered Johnno, who had reached the deck by now. "It'll drift away and pose a threat to other ships. Fetch my diving suit."

With his customary *sang froid*, Johnstone went down to the mine's cable and tried to disentangle it from the anchor chain. Once it bobbed to the surface, the crew would be able to blow it up with one well-aimed gunshot. (The *Claymore's* armaments consisted of two old rifles.) But, try as he might, Johnstone couldn't release the explosive orb. So, he marked its position with a wooden buoy, and Captain Williams reluctantly cut the anchor cable and sailed away. The *Claymore* returned to the mainland and persuaded a navy mine sweeper to accompany her on her next outing.

This was only one of several encounters the *Claymore* had with mines. But the navy refused to take the ragbag crew and their scruffy tub seriously, not even allowing them a ship-to-shore radio in case of emergency. They steadfastly refused to sweep the whole area, hoping that the salvage team would get the message they were in dangerous waters and leave.

But the *Claymore* and her crew were tougher than they looked. They continued the search, through winter storms and weeks of ceaseless work, until, on January 31, 1941, they struck a large object on the seabed. This time, Johnstone's report from the bell made Captain Williams clap his hands with delight.

"He can see her," he boomed to the crew. "We've found the *Niagara*."

There were wild celebrations in the crew rooms that week, but the mood in the captain's quarters was less jubilant. Williams and his divers knew the hardest part of the job was still ahead of them.

"She's in the mud, said Johnstone, who had completed his initial observation dives. "And she's lying at an angle of 70°."

"That's bad," sighed Williams. "The deck floor in the strongroom was made of reinforced steel, but the walls were weak. If the gold's fallen against them it might have dropped through into another part of the ship."

"Well, skipper," replied Johnstone with a smile. "I suppose we'll have to see for ourselves."

Their first job was to sink the concrete mooring blocks in a circle on the seabed, at a radius from the wreck of 244m (800 feet). Each block weighed as much as a truck and the *Claymore* listed heavily as she ferried them out from the mainland. Because steel buoys were so hard to come by, the salvage team used huge *kauri* logs from the New Zealand forests, to act as markers for the blocks. This exotic wood is as hard as iron and can be used underwater for years before it starts to rot.

It took until April 5, 1941, to position the blocks, cables and buoys and begin blasting. Williams and his divers had been busy memorizing every single detail of the wreck, so they could communicate effectively between bell and bridge. To get to the strongroom, they planned to remove a cone shape from the wreck's side, with its tapering point right at the room's entrance. This opening would only be a few feet across, just wide enough to permit the grab. After each blast, they would remove any debris and dump it on the sea floor. In order to plot the explosions accurately, the divers – and Williams – had to know exactly where the bell was on the wreck.

Johnno made a cardboard model of the *Niagara*, and studied it for weeks. He designed a special code of letters and numerals, so that Williams knew the deck, room, and even which porthole his diver was describing. This "language" between the captain and his divers had to be understood quickly and precisely. There were no underwater cameras or close-circuit televisions to help the salvage team. Williams used his imagination to visualize where the bell was, and how to lower the charge so the diver could monitor it. When the code worked well, Williams could drop the charge cable to within a few inches of the bell's observation windows.

On some days the clarity of the water was astounding, "like an aquarium," said Johnno. But, for most of the dives, visibility was a problem. The Johnstones had to press their faces up to the glass, checking that the charge cable was in the correct position, before rising to the surface in preparation for the blast. Sometimes when they were peering into the gloom, an eel would rush out of the darkness at the bell. These animals had bodies as thick as giant anacondas and heads the size of a cat's. There were many nervous moments down in the silence of the deep.

It could take up to three hours to place a charge, so progress was slow. But the team understood the importance of patience with this kind of work. The gold was buried 8m (26 feet) inside the heart of the ship. They had to smash their way through thousands of kilograms of steel and wood to get to their target, and each charge had to produce the correct explosive force. As they worked their way deeper into the wreck, they reduced the power of the blasts, fearful that they might dislodge the gold.

On September 25, Johnno sighted the strongroom door. The team argued for hours about the size of the charge needed to remove this last obstacle to the treasure. When Johnno went down to survey the blast results, there was good news and bad. Although the room was open, he couldn't peer far inside it. Johnno could guide the grab in, but he couldn't see the gold.

For days, the grab brought up nothing but mud and scrap. Williams had designed the machine himself. It had razor-sharp steel jaws worked by three cables attached to the ship; it could cut and tear its way through any material. The captain ordered Johnno to keep sending the grab in, refusing to accept that the elusive gold might have crashed through one of the strongroom walls and slipped deeper into the wreck.

It was a stormy afternoon on October 14 when Johnno went down in the bell to do his shift. Time and again, he watched the steel pincers withdraw from the strongroom clutching nothing but lumps of steel and clods of mud. But, suddenly, as the grab rushed past the bell, he thought he saw a box protruding from its mouth.

"The grab's out," muttered Johnno, still puzzled by what he'd seen.

"Should we dump it?" asked the captain.

"I'm not sure," came the reply.

Williams couldn't control his voice. He knew Johnno must have spotted something unusual.

"What was it, man?" the captain hissed.

"I think it might be worth a look, that's all," replied Johnno. "I'm not making any promises. But I thought I saw a small box."

The bell and grab were drawn up at top speed. Johnno had clambered out and was waiting with the others when the grab's steel jaws finally broke water.

"There's something there," shouted a sailor.

"Bring it in carefully," ordered Williams.

The grab wheeled around over the deck and spat out a load of mud and debris – and a small wooden box. As it hit the planks the box crumbled and two heavy bars spilled out. They were glittering and untarnished, a shimmering yellow like the sun.

The *Claymore* had struck gold.

Captain Williams was a stubborn and determined man. He didn't want to leave one gold bar in the underwater vault of the *Niagara* unless he had to. But, nearly two months later, on December 8, 1941, he finally declared that the mission was over. The grab had scooped out 555 ingots, an incredible 94% of the original bullion. Only 35 bars had fallen deeper into the wreck, or been swallowed by the mud on the seabed. Throughout the operation the *Claymore* had been plagued by foul weather and constant problems with her mooring cables. But the salvage team had succeeded against all odds. Every man had shown patience and grit. On some days they had been lucky to raise one bar. On others, they had managed to lift 92 ingots out of the sea. It was a proud ship that steamed back to the mainland in mid-December. The banking officials waiting on the pier could hardly believe that this dirty old tramp steamer and her shabby crew had brought up a fountain of gold.

TRUE
ESCAPE
STORIES
Paul Dowswell

Finally, the night had come to take a trip to the roof. Morris spent the day beforehand trying to curb his restlessness. What if the way up to the roof was blocked? What if the ventilator motor had been replaced after all? All their painstaking work would be wasted. The 12-year sentence stretched out before him. Then another awful thought occurred. The holes in the wall would be discovered eventually, and that would mean even more years added on to his sentence.

As well as locked doors, high walls and barbed wire, many escaping prisoners also face savage dogs and armed guards who shoot to kill. From Alcatraz to Devil's Island, read the extraordinary tales of people who risked their lives for their freedom.

Also from Usborne True Stories

TRUE
SURVIVAL
STORIES
Paul Dowswell

As he fell through the floor Griffiths
instinctively grabbed at the bombsight
with both hands, but an immense gust of
freezing air sucked the rest of his body
out of the aircraft. With the wind and the
throb of the Boston's two engines
roaring in his ears, he found himself
halfway out of the plane, legs and lower
body pressed hard against the fuselage.
He yelled at the top of his voice:
"Geeeerrrooooowwww!!!!", but knew
immediately that there was almost no
chance his crewmate could hear him.

From shark attacks and blazing airships to exploding
spacecraft and sinking submarines, these are real
stories of people who have stared death in the face
and lived to tell the tale. Find out what separates the
living from the dead when catastrophe strikes.

Also from Usborne True Stories

TRUE STORIES
OF
HEROES

Paul Dowswell

His blood ran cold and Perevozchenko
was seized by panic. He knew that his
body was absorbing lethal doses of
radiation, but instead of fleeing he stayed
to search for his colleague. Peering into
the dark through a broken window, he
could see only a mass of tangled
wreckage. By now he had absorbed so
much radiation he felt his whole body
was on fire. But then he remembered that
there were several other men near to the
explosion who might be trapped...

From firefighters battling with a blazing nuclear
reactor to a helicopter rescue team on board a fast-
sinking ship, this is an amazingly vivid collection of
stories about men and women whose extraordinary
courage has captured the imagination of millions.

Shortlisted for the Blue Peter Book Awards 2002

Also from Usborne True Stories

TRUE
SPY
STORIES

Paul Dowswell & Fergus Fleming

"In all your years of fame," Kramer explained delicately, "you have known some of the most powerful men in Europe. Would you consider returning to Paris now to mingle again with these influential gentlemen? And, while you're doing this, might you be able to keep me informed of anything interesting they might say?"

Margaretha looked curious but non-committal.

Kramer went on, "We could pay you well for this information — say 24,000 francs."

What are real spies like? Some, like beautiful Mata Hari, are every bit as glamorous as famous fictional agents such as James Bond. But spies usually live shadowy double lives, risking prison, torture and execution for a chance to change history.

Also from Usborne True Stories

TRUE EVEREST ADVENTURES

Paul Dowswell

Tejbir collapsed soon afterwards, telling Finch and Bruce he had no strength to go on. Defeated, he returned to the tent. Then as Finch and Bruce climbed higher, a terrible wind blew up, making progress extremely slow. At 8,320m (27,300ft) disaster struck. Finch, who was leading the climb, suddenly heard Bruce call out in alarm: "I'm getting no oxygen!" Finch turned to see his companion wavering and about to topple off the mountain.

Everest has fascinated climbers ever since it was first discovered 150 years ago. Since then, over a thousand of them have stood triumphant on its summit. But the frozen bodies that litter its slopes tell another tale of tragedy, misfortune and reckless ambition.

TRUE
POLAR
ADVENTURES
Paul Dowswell

By day, they pushed on through towering seas, while men not rowing bailed furiously to keep their open boats afloat. By night, they clambered aboard passing ice floes, to shiver in their tents. But one night there was a loud crack, and the ice split through the middle of a tent. Ernest Holness, one of the *Endurance's* strokers, fell through. He floundered in the freezing sea, trapped in his soaking sleeping bag, stunned almost to paralysis by the shock of the icy water.

Guarded by frozen seas and vast fields of snow, the North and South poles are among the world's most mysterious places. But these bleak environments are no place for humans, as the explorers who set out to unearth their secrets have found to their cost.

Shortlisted for the Blue Peter Book Awards 2003